LEARNING IS CHANGE

MARTHA M. LEYPOLDT
JUDSON PRESS, Valley Forge

LEARNING IS CHANGE

International Standard Book No. 0-8170-0526-9

Library of Congress Catalog Card No. 70-144082

Printed in the U.S.A.

Contents

Introduction

One of the most exciting things that happened to me recently was my participation in a clay-sculpturing course at the Philadelphia Museum of Art. It was an educational experience: an illustration of experiential learning.

I was a complete novice at working with clay. The day that I enrolled in the class, I was introduced to the teacher, who is a short, slightly-built man about sixty years of age. He smiled at me, called me by name, and took me over to a large barrel filled with piles of clay. He asked me to take a chunk. He took some out for me and I took some. He then led me over to a small pedestal and placed his stack of clay on it, and I added mine. All he said to me was, "Play around with the clay, squash it, twist it, pound it, and see what will emerge, then refine." That's all he said, and then he left me on my own.

Going from person to person, as forms emerged from other lumps of clay, he made appropriate remarks to the students. These are some of the things he said:

Have patience!

You have to really care!

Let yourself go!

Don't be stiff!

Have patience!

It will be a struggle!

Love is not done with the head!

Let's look together!

As we were working he read a quotation by Rodin who said that sometimes he started with one thing and ended up with another. That is what our teacher was asking us to do. We were challenged to be creative!

After two hours of work, he asked us to stop and look at what the others had done. The first molded clay we viewed was made by a young mother who had fashioned her clay into the likeness of her young daughter. As we stood before it, the teacher said:

"When God made man, he took a lump of clay and molded it.

Then he blew in it the breath of life. That's what I'm looking for:

LIFE!

What we were trying to capture in the sculpturing course is what we are trying to capture in this book:

LIFE!!

That word expresses the purpose of experiential learning
— that you may live; and
— that you may assist others to live!

We are interested in zestful living!

It is a sorry state for the person who, on his deathbed, suddenly realizes that he has already been dead for many years —
he was a noncreative person.

I LOVE LIFE!

THIS BOOK IS ALIVE!

Let me invite you to live with it.

How to Read This Book

A person involved in experiential education contemplates and reflects on what that activity means to his life.

This kind of education is "real"
Because the learner is involved
And the learning which results is his.

He learns by reflecting —
He learns by doing —
He learns by being.

This book is designed as an exciting experience in learning. Reading it will not be just an academic exercise if you enter into the experience, and the learning will be yours if you participate wholly in the design of the book.

In addition to the main text of the book there are interspersed, at appropriate places, two kinds of activities:

1. *Reflections* are opportunities for you to reflect on experiences in your own life that relate to the material being presented. (Sometimes you will be invited to write down these reflections and share them with others.)

2. *Exercises* are opportunities for you to participate in some kind of activity. Sometimes the activity will be in the form of writing; sometimes physical activity will be involved. Some exercises are to be done alone and others involve two or more persons.

You will benefit most from the book if you participate in the reflection experiences and the exercises as they are placed in the book.

If, for some good reason, you are not interested in active involvement, the book is written so that you can read only the main script and you will be able to understand the message of the book. Perhaps you will need to do this the first time you read the book. Later, you can come back to the book and participate in the involving experiences.

Will you just read the book?
or
Will you become involved?

1
Who Is an Adult?

Are you an adult?

Is there any question in your mind whether or not you are an adults?

Have you ever considered what really constitutes adulthood?

This chapter should help you clarify your thinking on this matter.

(If you have chosen to read the book without becoming involved in the reflections or exercises, turn to page 8).

For your notes	REFLECTION 1
	This is an invitation to reminisce!

This is an invitation to reminisce!
Can you recall the experiences that seem to be the most significant events in your life?
Think!
Think!
Think!
Write down your thoughts on paper.
Share your thoughts with someone else.
Think specifically!
What was your happiest moment? What made it so?
What was your saddest moment? What made it so?
What was your most successful moment? What made it so?
What was your most miserable failure? What made it so?
What was a real turning point in your life? What made it so?
What was the time of greatest tension? What made it so?
What was the time of greatest freedom or release?
What made it so?

> *Think!*
>   *Think!*
>   *Think!*
>   *Write and/or share!*

For your notes	**REFLECTION 2**
	Now, stop and think again!
	At what time in your life did the above events take place?
	— when you were a child?
	— when you were a youth?
	— when you were an adult?
	Analyzing the time when the above events took place might help you to see your own life in a new perspective.

For your notes	**REFLECTION 3**
	Let us do some more probing!
	How did you determine the way you answered the question about the kinds of events that took place when you were an adult? What criteria did you use to determine when you became an adult?
	Think!
	Think!
	Write and/or share!
	Maybe this next question will make it easier for you to consider criteria.
	When did you feel that you became an adult?
	Think!
	Think!
	Write and/or share!
	Did you consider any of these events?

Listed below are experiences that various people have said were the turning points in their lives when they felt that they became adults.

— My first date alone with a person of the opposite sex.
— My first job.
— My first paycheck.
— When I entered the military service.
— When I graduated from high school.

— When I owned my first car.
— When I became twenty-one.
— When I registered to vote.
— When I became free of my parents.
— When I went away to college.
— When I took up my occupation.
— When I became engaged.
— When I married.
— When I graduated from college.
— When I established my own living quarters.
— When I was able to recognize hostility for what it was.

Most adults list more than one experience, but others pick only the most significant experience that determined when they thought they became adults, or when they felt as if they were adults. Since people answer differently, we see that determining who is an adult is not an easy matter.

We can, however, form some generalizations about an adult person.

Adulthood does not begin at a specific age. Some people use age as a criterion for adulthood. One definition of the beginning of adulthood is "the age of eighteen years." Until recent years many Christian educators have considered the age of twenty-five as the beginning of young adulthood. Recent developments, however, have brought this age down to approximately eighteen years or the time of graduation from high school. The United Presbyterian Church in the U.S.A. is considering the eleventh-grader as an adult. The trend seems to be in keeping with Edgar Friedenberg's thesis that adolescence is becoming a vanishing phenomenon.[1]

In contrast to this view, Gale Jensen and his associates state very emphatically that age is no criterion for adulthood.[2] There are difficulties in using age as a criterion. People vary to such a great extent in their maturing process — physically, mentally, socially, emotionally, morally, sexually, and spiritually — that it is difficult to categorize all people as reaching adulthood at the same age level.

Adulthood involves some degree of continuity and stability. By contrast, adolescence is a time of vacillation. One moment the adolescent may act like a child and the next moment he may act like an adult. In the process of growing up, the adolescent sometimes has an intense desire to be like an adult while at other times his desire is to be more childlike. Developing from dependence to independence involves some rugged experiences.

Although the adolescent may have felt that one experience at the age of sixteen, for instance, may have been an adult experience, becoming an adult does not take place in a "twinkling of an eye" or by some magic milestone in one's life. Each experience must be weighed in relation to his other experiences in order to determine whether or not he is an adult or is still in the adolescent stage of development. There must be some continuing experiences and some stability in them to classify oneself as having reached adulthood.

Adulthood involves assuming responsibilities. The kinds of transitional experiences that have been noted above all denote the assuming of some kind of responsibility, such as gainful employment, marriage, parenthood, or civic responsibilities. The beginning of adulthood, therefore, involves a series of transitional experiences which involve assuming responsibilities for one's own decisions and actions. These experiences will vary for the married and the unmarried person. An event that may be significant in one person's life may be insignificant for another.

Adulthood is a process of becoming. Becoming an adult does not mean that we have arrived. The beginning of adulthood is a process of becoming. Although some significant events make us feel like adults, for some people there is such a gradual process from adolescence to adulthood that nothing clearly distinguishes any climactic experiences. But throughout the period of adulthood this process of becoming continues.

If we use the criterion of physical maturity as a basis for determining adulthood, it is important to differentiate between being an adult and being mature. Here we are using the term "maturity" in a wider sense than the physical realm. Maturity, as we will refer to it, involves the full achievement of physiological, psychological, sociological, sexual, moral, mental, and spiritual potential. In this sense, maturity is never achieved, and adulthood, therefore, involves a maturing process.

Criteria for a Mature Adult.

Let us test out the concept of the process of maturing by examining our own lives by the following criteria which have been culled from a variety of resources.[3]

A mature adult:

1. Has the ability to deal constructively with reality, knowing "who he is" and "who he is not."

2. Realizes his own limitations, but thinks well of himself and his abilities without boasting or a sense of guilt.

3. Sees himself as a part of a world of social change and has the capacity to adjust to change.

4. Has the ability to accept things and people the way they are, rather than the way he wants them to be.

5. Has the ability to accept the leadership of others without rebellion or self-abdication.

6. Has the capacity to find more satisfaction in giving than receiving and, when receiving, to do it graciously.

7. Guides his actions by long-range goals rather than by immediate impulses.

8. Is able to recognize and admit his hostile feelings and direct them into creative and constructive outlets.

9. Is able to create a proper balance between work and play.

10. Has the capacity to love and to be loved.

11. Has the capacity to relate to other people in a consistent manner and to do unto others as he would have them do to him.

12. Has the ability to empathize with others, that is, to participate in another's feelings or ideas.

13. Has the ability to accept his own sex, and the opposite sex, and to develop a relation between the two in ways that are appropriately fulfilling.

14. Has the skill and freedom to communicate with others.

15. Has the ability to choose between alternative ways of behaving and to assume responsibility for his choices.

16. Is able to relate himself to a Being higher than himself.

EXERCISE 1

Are you willing to test your own maturity? If so, circle the number which represents most nearly your level of achievement in each category. (Refer to items above to clarify the meanings of these words.)

	Completely achieved			Partly achieved		Never achieved	
1. Reality	6	5	4	3	2	1	0
2. Self	6	5	4	3	2	1	0
3. Change	6	5	4	3	2	1	0
4. Acceptance	6	5	4	3	2	1	0
5. Leadership	6	5	4	3	2	1	0
6. Giving	6	5	4	3	2	1	0
7. Goals	6	5	4	3	2	1	0
8. Hostility	6	5	4	3	2	1	0

9. Work—play	6	5	4	3	2	1	0
10. Loving	6	5	4	3	2	1	0
11. Relating	6	5	4	3	2	1	0
12. Empathy	6	5	4	3	2	1	0
13. Sexuality	6	5	4	3	2	1	0
14. Communication	6	5	4	3	2	1	0
15. Responsibility	6	5	4	3	2	1	0
16. Spirituality	6	5	4	3	2	1	0

Now, total the numbers circled. Put your score here ☐. You are a **mature** adult and have fully arrived if you score a perfect 96 every time you take the test, today, one month from now, two months, etc., ad infinitum.

Are you still in the process of becoming?

Do you think it is possible for you to become fully mature?

Do you think it is possible for someone else to become fully mature?

Although the list states criteria for maturity, no person has the ability to achieve all of these qualities to the fullest. Therefore, we are constantly challenged to strive for maturity, and always need to engage in the process of becoming more mature.

Let us now consider the nature of spiritual maturity. When Paul wrote to the Ephesians, he stated:

It was he who "gave gifts to men": he appointed some to be apostles, others to be prophets, others to be evangelists, others to be pastors and teachers. He did this to prepare all God's people for the work of Christian service, to build up the body of Christ. And so we shall all come together to that oneness in our faith and in our knowledge of the Son of God; we shall become mature men, reaching to the very height of Christ's full stature (Ephesians 4:11-13, TEV).

For your notes	REFLECTION 4
	Are you willing to examine your own spiritual maturity? To what extent have you reached the very height of Christ's mature stature? Are you still in the process of becoming spiritually mature? Think of specific instances that will substantiate or repudiate your spiritual maturity.

Isn't it presumptuous of us to consider it possible for anyone to reach the height of Christ's mature stature? It would make us Christ. Spiritual maturity is an ideal, not a reality to be completely attained.

Paul, himself, in examining his life admitted:

> I do not claim that I . . . have already become perfect. I keep going on to try to possess it, for Christ Jesus has already possessed me. Of course, brothers, I really do not think that I have already reached it; the one thing I do, however, is to forget what is behind me and do my best to reach what is ahead. So I run straight toward the goal in order to win the prize, which is God's call through Christ Jesus to the life above (Philippians 3:12-14, TEV).

With the criteria for maturity before us, we are continually in the process of developing, becoming, or maturing. If this tension is substantiated in our life, we will always be confronted with a challenge. As we are striving toward the goal, we are developing, growing, becoming more mature. If we could "arrive," or achieve full maturity, we would be sterile, self-satisfied, and inactive. Therefore, we realize that God, in his infinite wisdom, has provided for the ongoing process of maturing.

As living organisms we are always in the process of developing. As spiritual beings we are always in the process of becoming.

An adult, therefore, is one whose transitional experiences from adolescence to adulthood have some continuity and stability, and whose life involves the assumption of the primary responsibilities for his own living. His experiences involve the struggle of the continuous process of becoming.

STAGES OF ADULTHOOD

There are three stages in this period of adulthood toward which all of life moves: young adulthood, middle adulthood, and senior adulthood. Earl Zeigler calls these stages: beginning adulthood, continuing adulthood, and arriving adulthood.[4] Each has its own characteristic experiences. We may list these experiences in a manner that allows for individual interpretation according to one's own observations and experiences.

WHO IS THE YOUNG ADULT?

LOVE IS . . .
by You

YOUNG
ADULTHOOD
IS . . .
by You

EXERCISE 2

The book **Happiness Is a Warm Puppy** contains many definitions of happiness. Each is a brief statement listed on the left-hand page, which is described by an appropriate picture on the right-hand page. Maybe you have seen this book or a book of similar format entitled, **Security**

Is a Warm Blanket, or others entitled, **Love Is . . . A Friend Is . . .**

We challenge you to make a book of your own, either alone or with a group. Entitle the book: **Young Adulthood Is . . . !**

Think!

Reminisce!

Share!

Write and Draw!

Compare your definitions with the ones listed below.

Here are some examples:
— Young adulthood is cut-off apron strings.
— Young adulthood is dreaming.
— Young adulthood is making decisions.
— Young adulthood is telephone calls.
— Young adulthood is promises.
— Young adulthood is a stack of books.
— Young adulthood is stretching a paycheck.
— Young adulthood is business ventures.
— Young adulthood is getting a promotion.
— Young adulthood is sleepless nights.
— Young adulthood is a new social group.

WHO IS THE MIDDLE ADULT?

EXERCISE 3

Now that you have had an experience in making a book, how about making another one, but entitle it: **Middle Adulthood Is . . . !**

Compare your definitions with the ones listed below.

Here are some examples:
— Middle adulthood is receding hairlines.
— Middle adulthood is empty chairs.
— Middle adulthood is new roles.
— Middle adulthood is promotions.
— Middle adulthood is new business ventures.
— Middle adulthood is bifocals.
— Middle adulthood is three-level families.

— Middle adulthood is letter writing.
— Middle adulthood is committees.
— Middle adulthood is organizations.
— Middle adulthood is traveling.
— Middle adulthood is golf.
— Middle adulthood is menopause.

WHO IS THE SENIOR ADULT?

SENIOR
ADULTHOOD
IS . . .

by You

EXERCISE 4

Making your third book is now in order.
Entitle this one: **Senior Adulthood Is . . . !**
Compare your definitions with the ones
listed below.

Here are some examples:
— Senior adulthood is grandchildren.
— Senior adulthood is hobbies.
— Senior adulthood is memories.
— Senior adulthood is remembering.
— Senior adulthood is forgetting.
— Senior adulthood is looking ahead.
— Senior adulthood is new friendships.
— Senior adulthood is adjustments.
— Senior adulthood is meaning.
— Senior adulthood is spiritual revitalization.
— Senior adulthood is mellowing.
— Senior adulthood is fulfillment.
— Senior adulthood is experiencing.

Each stage of adulthood has its own struggles and its own
rewards. Adulthood lived with a purpose is ecstasy. God breathed
into man the breath of life. When man acknowledges and accepts life as a gift, he gives thanks and uses it for God's glory.

Adulthood is the exciting process of continually becoming —
a process which involves:
— an ever-increasing sense of being a person of worth to oneself,
to others, and to God,
— an ever-increasing awareness of and assuming responsibility
for being God's agent for reconciliation in a troubled world.
Adulthood is becoming — becoming — becoming —
not
having arrived.

2
Teacher/Leader, Who Are You?

A broad concept of a teacher is used in this book. A teacher includes any person who assumes a leadership role in a group of persons, who assists a group to achieve the goals which they have set for themselves. When the word "teacher" is used, the word "group leader" can be substituted in its place and the word "learner" can also be replaced by the word "group member" in any situation where such changes would be appropriate.

Meet Mr. X

Mr. X has taught a class of adults for many years. Each Sunday he lectures to his class. He is quite satisfied with his way of teaching and assumes that his students are also satisfied because they continue to come.

Mr. X thinks that a teacher is an instructor who must talk — talk — talk.

Mr. X thinks that a teacher is the only possessor of knowledge.

Mr. X thinks that the only way that students learn is to listen — listen — listen.

Mr. X is like a sifter which allows only the kind of material it wants to pass through it.

Meet Mr. A

Mr. A seldom lectures. He realizes that a lecture is only one of many methods which a teacher can utilize. He believes that a variety of methods is the key. He thinks that his task as a teacher is to provide meaningful learning experiences for his students, so he gives them opportunity to become involved in the teaching◄► learning process. (The symbol◄► pictures the cooperative, interactive nature of the teaching◄► learning task.)

Mr. A may not know it, but he agrees with Ralph Tyler who says that it is what the student does that he learns, and not what the teacher does.[1]

Mr. A is like a refreshing rain that provides stimulus for growth and response from all that it touches.

Mr. A thinks of teaching as a very different kind of a task than Mr. X does.

EXERCISE 5

Think of one of your church school teachers. Finish the sentence:

My teacher is like . . .

Write as many similes as you wish.

EXERCISE 6

Think of the teacher who has had the greatest influence on your life. Finish the sentence:

This teacher is like . . .

Write as many similes as you like.

Mr. X may need to develop:
— new ways of looking at his task;
— new ways of teaching;
— new ways of preparing for his teaching task; and
— new kinds of skills for greater variety.

Mr. X may also need a better understanding of how adults learn and what learning is.

Mr. A is the kind of teacher I want to describe and the kind of teacher that I hope you will become. Therefore, I will describe characteristics of Mr. A. In the left-hand margin I will list the characteristics of a teacher who provides experiences for his students that are meaningful and that produce change in himself and his students. On the right-hand side are some illustrations of those characteristics in action.

1. *A teacher is a change-agent.*

1. Mr. A is open to change. He assists his students to change while he himself is willing to change.

2. *A teacher is a learner.*

2. Mr. A knows that in this day when there is such a vast accumulation of knowledge, he cannot know everything. He lets his students know that he is learning with them. In this way, Mr. A can make mistakes without being embarrassed about it. Nor is he embarrassed to learn from his students, for together they are searching for truth.

3. *A teacher is a resource person.*

3. Mr. A looks for many resources by which his students may learn for themselves. He also makes himself available to his students as they search for specific areas

of knowledge that he alone may be able to give or to suggest the places where some answers may be found.

4. *A teacher is a person.*

4. Mr. A is a person with feelings, desires, and needs like any other person in his class. He has the same need for love, acceptance, and belonging that his students have. He wants his students to think of him as a person rather than a dispenser of knowledge.

5. *A teacher is a listener.*

5. Mr. A tries to understand his students. In order to do so he listens to what they have to say — their desires, their hopes, their frustrations, their questions. Mr. A also wants to be sure that his students understand what he is saying, so he listens to them as they respond to him. Meanings are clarified when necessary.

6. *A teacher is one who loves.*

6. Mr. A LOVES LIFE. He tackles his task with enthusiasm, with purpose, and with hope.

Mr. A LOVES GOD. He experiences the love of God in his own life and desires to share this love with others.

Mr. A LOVES HIMSELF. He accepts the teaching of Jesus when he said: "Love your neighbor as yourself." He knows that he must have confidence in himself if he is to teach others. He has to have enough self-confidence so that he can admit that he is wrong without destroying his integrity as a person. Mr. A feels that his love of self is in response to God's regard for every person as a person of worth. If he does not think of himself as worthy, it will be hard for others to think of him in this way.

Mr. A also LOVES OTHERS. He uses the thirteenth chapter of First Corinthians for his guide because it describes the qualities of a person who loves God and others. (The following description of love is based upon 1 Corinthians 13 in Today's English Version.)

Love is
patient.

Mr. A realizes that because change is often difficult, patience is necessary. He is willing to wait until people are ready to change.

Love is *kind.*

Mr. A is friendly and shows by his acts that he is concerned about the persons in his class.

Love is *trust.*

(Love is not jealous.)

Mr. A feels that trust is basic to any relationship, so he trusts his students. Since they are aware of his trust, they also trust him.

Love is
modest.
(Love is not conceited:
love is not proud.)

Mr. A knows a great deal about the subjects that he teaches but he does not flaunt this knowledge to his students. He knows that students learn more when they discover things for themselves.

Love is *polite.*
(Love is not ill-mannered.)

Mr. A has regard for persons with other points of view than his own. He listens to what they have to say and tries to understand their point of view.

Love is
generous.
(Love is not selfish.)

Mr. A gives of himself and his possessions as an act of love on appropriate occasions. He finds that what he gives to others comes back to him in many ways that are rewarding.

Love is *calm.*
(Love is not irritable.)

Mr. A is calm when difficult situations arise and other persons are emotionally involved. He gives assurance of love and concern for persons in time of crisis. He is calm when persons make mistakes and when persons are slow in responding.

Love is *positive*.
(Love does not keep record of wrongs.)

Mr. A thinks the best of persons rather than the worst. He tries to forget the wrongs that others have done. He does not hold a grudge, but is forgiving.

Love is *good*.
(Love is not happy with evil.)

Mr. A shows love and acceptance to persons who have done wrong without knowing what they have done.

Love is *truth*.
(Love is happy with truth.)

Mr. A is searching continually for truth. He is joyful when he achieves the satisfaction of having accomplished something worthwhile. He rejoices with others who have this same feeling of accomplishment.

Love is *persistence*.
(Love never gives up.)

Mr. A continues to love persons who do wrong to him or to others. He accepts these persons' actions, though they be irksome, realizing that they have reasons for behaving as they do. He feels strongly that loving rather than judging brings healing to persons' lives.

Love is *faith*.
(Love will never fail.)

Mr. A believes that faith in himself, in other persons, and in God is basic to all relationships.

Love is *hope*.
(Love has hope.)

Mr. A is optimistic that persons can learn. His hope for the growth of others as well as himself gives him the ability to continue with a difficult task.

Love is *eternal.*	Mr. A has the assurance that amid the turmoil of change, love is one thing that does not change. Regardless of time or situations, love brings healing.
7. *A teacher is a friend.*	7. Mr. A is willing to give and take in intimate relationships with members of his class.
8. *A teacher is an enabler.*	8. Mr. A feels that he has an enabling ministry. He enables others to function effectively. He enables others who are in difficulty to accept themselves and work through their problems to some fulfilling conclusion.
9. *A teacher is a reflector.*	9. Mr. A reflects on the words of others. He states in his own words what he thinks others are saying. He reflects on the feelings of others, trying to understand why a person feels the way he does.

EXERCISE 7

Ask a person in the group or class to make a statement, then respond to him:

Do I understand you to say . . . (and in your own words repeat what you think he has said). Continue the dialogue until you have a meeting of meanings.

10. *A teacher is a provider.*	10. Mr. A provides the resources, the setting, the equipment, the physical conditions, and the kinds of learning experiences appropriate for learning. He also provides information but realizes that the more a student seeks out his own information the more he will learn.
11. *A teacher is an explorer.*	11. Mr. A explores new ways of approaching life, of approaching truth, of approaching the Bible. He leaves no stone unturned in his continuing search for truth.
12. *A teacher is a responder.*	12. Mr. A realizes that every action, every word, every attitude, every movement has meaning. He responds appropriately to each in a manner that will produce under-

standing and will translate it into meaningful words, attitudes, or actions. His students know that he cares.

The learner initiates by word, attitude, and action;

the teacher responds in a constructive fashion.

13. *A teacher is a motivator.*

13. Mr. A provides conditions and opportunities so that his students will want to learn. He gives an encouraging word, an encouraging smile, a nod of the head, a gentle pat on the shoulder, or a squeeze of the hand when appropriate in order to open the door for learning.

14. *A teacher is a delegater.*

14. Mr. A delegates responsibilities to others rather than doing all the work himself.

15. *A teacher is a sensitizer.*

15. Mr. A is sensitive to other persons and assists others to be sensitive. He is not easily hurt but is aware of other persons' needs, abilities, and limitations. He knows when people need support and he gives it to them. He also knows when people can accept direct confrontation of some error, and he knows how to confront the person without degrading him.

16. *A teacher is an empathizer.*

16. Mr. A is able to enter imaginatively into the lives of his students and feel as if their experiences were his own. He tries to think as they think and tries to feel as they feel.

EXERCISE 8

Think of a person who has a problem. Perhaps it will be a person with whom you disagree or whom you dislike very much. Try to think as this person thinks and feel as this person feels about a particular issue or problem.

EXERCISE 9

When two persons in your class strongly disagree, ask each of them to take the opposite point of view and imagine that they are the other person.

17. *A teacher is a pray-er.*

17. Mr. A realizes his need of divine power and wisdom. He prays for himself and for those in his care. He makes his prayers specific.

18. *A teacher is an experimenter.*

18. Mr. A is never satisfied with what he is doing, or with what others have done in the past. He is willing to see things in new perspectives and try new ways of thinking, new ways of feeling, and new ways of acting.

19. *A teacher is a risker.*

19. Mr. A is willing to risk, realizing that he may fail, but always hoping and working that he will gain new insights regardless of the outcome.

20. *A teacher is an evaluator.*

20. Mr. A is continually evaluating himself and others. He sets goals for himself and evaluates outcomes in relation to these goals. He evaluates the forces that are at work in the class as persons respond to each other. He also assists others to grow in their ability to evaluate these forces at work.

EXERCISE 10

Below are listed some postures of a teacher. Study them carefully and note those that you consider helpful to real learning. Study them in the light of the characteristics mentioned above and put a "+" before the items that assist learning and a "—" before the items that deter learning.

1. Sitting at a table around which students sit.
2. Standing while students sit.
3. Walking among students as they study.
4. Sitting on a desk while teaching.
5. Sitting or standing on a raised platform.
6. Sitting behind a desk while teaching.
7. Talking from the back of the room.
8. Sitting in a special chair.
9. Sitting on a high stool.
10. Standing behind a podium.
11. Actively gesturing while pupils are still.
12. Looking directly at students.[2]

Suggested answers:

+: 1, 3, 12   —: 2, 4, 5, 6, 7, 8, 9, 10, 11

An effective teacher is concerned with change in himself and others. He is a learner with his students. His task is that of providing meaningful learning experiences for his students so that they can explore new meanings, feelings, and actions within a supportive climate. He opens doors so that others will see opportunities that are new and realize potentials within themselves of which they are not aware. He learns how to open doors and when to open them.

3
What Is Learning?

Meet Mr. B

Mr. B is teaching a class of young adults and is puzzled about how he should do so. At first he lectured to the young adults, and he wondered why they lacked interest. Attendance declined; so he decided to quit. The church school superintendent talked with him about it.

"Would you like to know why the class members don't respond?" the superintendent queried.

"I surely would!" replied Mr. B with eager anticipation.

"You are the one who is doing the learning and not the students. You don't allow them to learn. You just tell them and that is only one way by which you can assist adults to learn. In fact, many times it is the least effective."

Two questions need to be asked: When have adults learned? What is learning? The answers to these questions will assist teachers to know what their task is.

WHEN HAVE ADULTS LEARNED?

Ralph Tyler says that a student learns through his active behavior. He learns through what he does and not through what the teacher does.[1]

(Mr. B did not know this. He did the opposite of what Dr. Tyler states. Mr. B thought that what he was doing was the most important thing. He did not know what students should be doing in order to learn.)

In what kinds of activities do students participate as they learn?

1. Students *listen.*[2]

(Mr. B already knew about this activity of the learner. Most teachers do. But Mr. B did not help his students to become engrossed with the gospel, experiencing and knowing it. He failed to motivate the learners to discover and appropriate meanings and values.)

2. Students *respond.*

(Mr. B found that some students responded but most of them did not. He did not provide occasions for them to respond by their assuming personal and social responsibility for the gospel.)

3. Students *explore.*

(*Mr. B did not allow his students to explore. He did all of the exploring and did not encourage his students to read, observe at first hand, interview others, or share in common experiences.*)

4. Students *discover.*

(*Since Mr. B's students hadn't done any exploring, how could they have discovered anything? He did not assist them to identify, reflect on, systematize, and test meanings and values.*)

5. Students *appropriate personally.*

(*Little of this was done in Mr. B's class. He did not help the students to interpret personal meaning and value in the light of the gospel, to make decisions between values, or to identify with persons.*)

6. Students *assume responsibility.*

(*Little learning took place in Mr. B's class; so the members had little or nothing for which to be responsible in terms of carrying out and evaluating projects.*)

(*Obviously Mr. B himself has a lot of learning to do in order to help his students to learn.*)

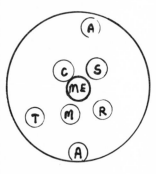

EXERCISE 11

Draw a large circle on a piece of paper. In the center of the circle draw a small circle and label it "ME." Draw other circles that represent people who have influenced your life. Put those who have had the greatest influence upon you closest to the center, and those who have had least influence near the circumference.

Now look at the diagram, and

REFLECT!

The people drawn in your circle represent your teachers, although some might not have considered themselves in this role. Reflect on how they influenced you. How do you feel about them?

What have they taught you?
What have you learned from them?
How did you learn from them?
What was your activity as a learner?

WHAT IS LEARNING?

To learn is to change!
Learning is changing!

When a person has learned, he is a changed person: he is transformed. This makes teaching exciting and should make learning exciting and alive.

(Mr. B will change as he learns. His students will change as he assists them to learn.)

When learning takes place, we change our entire person. As one aspect of our being changes, it affects other aspects of our being, making us different persons. We are not compartmentalized into physical, mental, emotional, psychological, and spiritual entities: we are one person with various facets of being. As we change, our heart as well as our mind is transformed.[3]

The term "change" is appropriate within a Christian context.
— Christian faith changes people.
— The Christian experience is one of productive change.
— The Christian experience is expanding and growing.
Paul's statement challenges us to change.

Therefore, my brothers, I implore you by God's mercy to offer your very selves to him: a living sacrifice, dedicated and fit for his acceptance, the worship offered by mind and heart. Adapt yourselves no longer to the pattern of this present world, but let your minds be remade and your whole nature thus transformed (Romans 12:1-2, NEB).

EXERCISE 12

Learning is
like
eating a juicy
apple.

Finish the following sentence.
Learning is like . . .
Write as many similes as you would like.
Now reflect whether your experiences of learning have been pleasurable, indifferent, frustrating, or a mixture of several or all.

WHAT KINDS OF CHANGES?

Three kinds of changes are involved in making us new persons:
— knowing
— feeling
— doing.[4]
We will look at each kind of change separately although all three are very much interrelated.

1. *Learning is changing our minds by adding new information.*

There are different levels of knowing; some involve very simple ways of knowing and others are more complex. From the simplest to the most complex these levels of knowing are:

To *recall* information received.

(Mr. B gives out information and expects his students to recognize and recall what he is saying. He thinks that his success as a teacher depends upon the students giving back the information he gave in the same way that he gave it. Mr. B is not aware that he is working at the simplest and lowest level of knowing. If Mr. B would want more "knowing" to take place, he would encourage his students to go to the more complex levels listed below.)

To *react* to and try to *understand* what the teacher and others are saying.

To *apply* this information to specific situations to see if understanding has really taken place.

To *analyze* what is involved in this new information.

To *evaluate* the new information to see if it has meaning to life.[5]

(Mr. B needs to try some of the other levels of "knowing" if he wants more effective learning to take place.)

Your goals	REFLECTION 5
	Examine the manner in which you teach. Does your teaching seek to encourage learning on the simplest or a more complex level? Does your teaching need some improvement in the knowing area? If so, set some definite goals for yourself.

2. *Learning is changing our feelings about ideas, things, persons, and circumstances.*

Feeling involves an attitude toward what is happening: it is different from emotions which involve the impulse of the moment. Feeling involves the sensitive awareness of ideas, persons, and things. It also involves valuing and commitment to values. There would be no meaning without feeling which is a pulse of life that encompasses our entire being.[6]

Adults feel deeply. They have values that they dearly cherish. They are committed to specific persons, ideas, and ideals. As teachers we need to recognize and appreciate these feelings. Some feelings need to be retained, some need to be refined, and others need to be changed.

As teachers it is imperative that we give more significance to learners' feelings since all learning begins on the feeling level.

A person accepts information if he feels disposed to accept it; he rejects information if he feels so disposed. When facts are presented to a person who has strong negative feelings about an

A person accepts information if he feels disposed to accept it; issue, the facts will be rejected until his feelings are changed.

The feeling level needs most of our attention since upon it will depend whether or not a person learns.

(Mr. B does not realize how important feelings are to adult learning. He is only concerned about adding new information and does not realize that he needs to be concerned with feelings if learning is to take place.)

3. *Learning is changing our actions.*

Changing our actions may mean changing our way of doing the things which we are now doing or doing entirely different kinds of things. Changes of actions are usually accomplished by following these certain steps:

Being *aware* of possible alternative actions.

Evaluating each alternative action.

Foreseeing consequences of each alternative.

Selecting an appropriate action on the basis of a value system.

Assuming the responsibility of accepting the consequences of new actions.

(Mr. B did not consider this aspect of learning.)

LEARNING IS — — — —

Since we define learning as changing, we can attribute the following characteristics to learning:

Learning is active.	It involves movement. Movement may be in the same or the reverse direction of present movement or goals.
Learning is experiencing.	It involves the entire being.
Learning is dynamic.	It has forceful motion.
Learning is discovery.	It is a discovery of self, persons, feelings, knowledge, and new ways of behaving.
Learning is vital.	Life cannot exist without it.
Learning is growth.	It is directed toward some desired end.

Learning is self-realization.	It involves self-fulfillment.
Learning is creative tension.	Tensions bring possibilities of choices.
Learning is meaning.	Life has value.
Learning is insight.	It brings the "aha" feeling.
Learning is involvement.	It includes both giving of oneself and receiving the giving of others.
Learning is self-revolution.	We are changed persons.
Learning is meeting of meanings.	We understand the meanings of others and they understand our meanings.
Learning is unfreezing.	From a frozen state we become fluid so we can change.[7]
Learning is ecstatic.	The time of learning is a moment of delight.[8]
Learning is what is happening now.	The change is now, not in the past or in the future. The past will have had a significant part in the learning experiences, and the consequences of learning will affect the future.
Learning is becoming.	The new person has the potential for future newness.

LEARNING IS CHANGING

Learning is making me a new person. Since learning involves change, we are different persons when we have learned. We are different persons when we have added new information; we are different persons when we have changed our attitudes, and we are different persons when we have changed our actions.

As Christians, our objective is to respond in faith and love to the person of Jesus Christ. (See page 34 for a complete statement of this objective.) This means changes in our lives as we are continuously becoming new persons in Jesus Christ. This means that life will continually have significant meanings.

4
What Changes Are Desired?

Meet Mr. C

When Mr. C was asked to teach a class of middle adults, he quickly agreed. His idea of teaching was that he wouldn't have to prepare a lesson, but would let the students decide each Sunday what they wanted to talk about. He was disappointed in the response of the class members when he tried this procedure. Some students did not like the approach and refused to come. Some students were enthusiastic at first but after a while one member of the class expressed what the others were thinking: "There doesn't seem to be any purpose in our class."

Mr. C needs assistance in bringing some purpose to his class. First of all, he needs to realize the importance of having goals or having a purpose for a learning experience.

Life must have a purpose if it is to have meaning. A group of people coming together to learn must have a purpose if their gathering is to be meaningful.

We will think of purpose, or having goals, in terms of:

WHAT KINDS OF CHANGES ARE DESIRED?

We are not interested in change for the sake of change; but we are interested in:

Change

with or for

a purpose.

We need to think of the three kinds of changes when we think of goals.

　　—Changes in knowing.
　　— Changes in feeling.
　　— Changes in doing.

Most teachers are only concerned with the desired changes in things to be known. All teachers need to consider all three kinds of changes when they are teaching.

(Mr. C did not consider any of these changes.)

Let us suggest some goals that Mr. C might consider at some time in his teaching. Look at them carefully to examine what they are saying. Three suggested goals will be given: one in the area of knowing, one in the area of feeling, and one in the area of doing. Try to identify the kind of change to which each of these goals apply.

Goal 1. To appreciate the various degrees of meaning used to interpret and communicate the Christian faith.

Goal 2. To understand the nature of our being as a part of the natural order of creation.

Goal 3. To confront the nature of our sinfulness and ask God's forgiveness.

	EXERCISE 13
Verb(s) denoting "knowing":	What kinds of changes are indicated in the statements of the above goals?
Verb(s) denoting "feeling":	Underline the infinitives in the statements. Examine these infinitives, for they are words that denote action or desired changes. What kinds of action are implied?
Verb(s) denoting "doing":	Categorize each infinitive into one of the three areas: knowing, feeling, or doing. (You may need to attach the adjoining phrase to the verb in order to categorize it correctly.)

In examining the infinitive verbal forms which are used in the above goals, we can determine the kinds of changes that are desired.

The verb in the first goal is
"appreciate."

This denotes a change in the *"feeling."*

The verb in the second goal is
"understand."

This denotes a change in the *"knowing."*

There are two verbs in the third goal. The first verb is
"confront."

The second verb is
"ask."

Both of these verbs denote changes in the "doing." The goal is stated so that we are hoping to do more than talk about forgiveness; that we will act with our entire being — heart, soul, strength, and mind (cf. Luke 10:27).

(The goals listed above would give direction and meaning to Mr. C's class experiences.)

EXERCISE 14

Your goal?

If you are a teacher of an adult class, what is the goal for your next teaching session?

If you have a teacher's guide, look for the goal of the session. Does it sound reasonable for the group of students in your class? If not, reword it as it relates appropriately to your specific group. Write this goal down on paper or in the boxed space provided here.

Underline the verb(s) in your stated goal and categorize them according to "knowing," "feeling," and "doing" areas. Which areas are stated?

In examining the goal in this way, are you satisfied with your statement of the kinds of desired changes? If not, rewrite the goal.

EXERCISE 15

No.

"knowing" verbs ☐

"feeling" verbs ☐

"doing" verbs ☐

Look through your entire teacher's guide. Examine every goal that is listed throughout the book.

Underline all of the verbs, and then fit them into one of the three categories: knowing, feeling, or doing.

How many verbs are in the "knowing" area?

How many verbs are in the "feeling" area?

How many verbs are in the "doing" area?

As we examine many teachers' guides, we find that there is a predominance of "knowing" goals and an exclusion or sparseness of "feeling" and "doing" goals. What does this say about our teaching? The teachers who are concerned primarily with teaching facts are missing some of the most vital teaching moments. The teachers who are concerned with all three areas — knowing, feeling, and doing — are the ones who will be seeing changes take place in persons.

When such changes do take place, true learning has occurred.

AN OVERALL GOAL

Now let us examine another goal. We will look closely at one statement of the objective of the church's educational ministry. It is a statement that describes the kinds of changes that need to be made through the educational program of the church.

> The objective for Christian education is that all persons be aware of God through his self-disclosure, especially his redeeming love as revealed in Jesus Christ, and that they respond in faith and love—to the end that they may know who they are and what their human situation means, grow as sons of God rooted in the Christian community, live in the Spirit of God in every relationship, fulfill their common discipleship in the world, and abide in the Christian hope.[1]

In order to examine the statement more carefully, let us restate this goal slightly so that we may identify the kinds of changes that we can expect to happen in persons.

1. To *aware* of God, through his self-disclosure, especially his redeeming love as revealed in Jesus Christ.

        — enabled by the Holy Spirit —

2. To *respond* in faith and love.
3. To *become* new persons in Christ.
4. To *know* who we are and what our human situation means.
5. To *grow* as sons of God rooted in the Christian community.
6. To *live* in obedience to the will of God in every relationship.
7. To *fulfill* our common vocation in the world.
8. To *abide* in the Christian hope.

Let us examine the verbs which are italicized.

EXERCISE 16

	Totals
Knowing	☐
Feeling	☐
Doing	☐

Below are three columns which are headed by the names of the three areas in which change takes place. Write in the appropriate column the verb in each of the eight goals listed above. Add the number of verbs in each column and write the totals in the boxes on the left.

Knowing	Feeling	Doing

Now look below to see how we have categorized the kinds of changes.

Looking at the above eight italicized verbs which indicate the kinds of changes desired, we may classify them in the following way:

Knowing	Feeling	Doing
4. to know	1. to be aware of 8. to abide	2. to respond 3. to become 5. to grow 6. to live 7. to fulfill

You might have wanted to classify some of the words differently from the way in which they are listed above. We have listed them in the area that we think is predominant. A word being categorized in one column does not mean that the other kinds of changes are completely eliminated in the one concept. For example, you may wish to put the change "to be aware of" in the "knowing" column. Certainly the aspect of knowing is involved in "being aware," but we believe this action is primarily on the feeling level because it involves an attitude toward something.

It is interesting to note that in the eight kinds of changes,

— only *one* is listed in the *knowing* area;
— *two* are listed in the *feeling* area; and
— *five* are listed in the *doing* area.

If we believe that these are our goals, our teaching should reflect these anticipated changes. If most of our teaching emphasizes the accumulation of facts, it is *not* in keeping with the main objective of the teaching ministry of the church. This means that we need to stress the "feeling" and "doing" levels to a greater extent.

WHO DETERMINES THE KINDS OF CHANGES?

There are four possible ways that we might approach the question as to who is to determine the kinds of changes to take place in persons who are learning together in a group. Let us look at them and examine the implications of each alternative.

Alternative 1. Individual goal-setting.

The student alone determines the kinds of changes that he would desire to happen.

The teacher who does not think that he has any responsibility for determining goals is being irresponsible. Although, in the long run, the student is the one to determine his own goals, individuals benefit from a community experience and interchange of ideas in bringing new insights into perspective.

(Mr. C has selected this alternative.)

Alternative 2. Dependent goal-setting.

The teacher feels that it is his sole responsibility to determine the kinds of changes which should take place in his students.

This alternative puts the teacher in complete control of the learning experience. The teacher works in an authoritarian manner when he alone determines the kinds of changes which should take place in his students. He assumes he has the final truth. Although he may not realize it, he is working under the assumption that he knows his students well and knows what is best for them and knows how they should change. He is probably taking for granted that all students have the same needs. He also assumes that students will consider him as an authority and will accept the goals which he defines.

This method of determining goals is for the insecure students who are not mature enough to want to do their own thinking and do not want to take any initiative for the learning experience. This method is also for the insecure teacher since it is the safest and easiest way to teach. The teacher is not threatened because he is in control.

Alternative 3. Cooperative goal-setting for students.

The teacher and the students are partners in determining the kinds of changes that should take place in the students.

Since most adults are responsible people and want to be treated as such, they ought to have an opportunity to assist in determining their own goals. The teacher who follows this course of action recognizes that persons who determine their own goals will be more apt to achieve these goals than if goals were imposed upon them.

Alternative 4. Cooperative goal-setting for students and teacher.

The teacher and the students are partners in determining the kinds of changes that should take place in both teacher and students.

In this kind of a procedure, the teacher does not assume that he knows all the truth and has all the answers; nor does he need to know all the answers. He is a person who is searching for truth along with his students. He has faith in his students and realizes that some of them may know more about some areas of inquiry, or may have deeper insights into some aspects of the problem, than he does. Such a teacher is willing to accept this situation without being threatened as a person.

This procedure is applicable for use with persons who are secure and eager to learn. A teacher may be desirous of working cooperatively but his students may not be ready for this kind of experience. He may need to begin at the level of the second or third alternative and then work gradually with his students to the point of cooperative goal-setting.

EXERCISE 17

Which of the four ways listed above is your style of developing goals?

To what extent is this style effective?

Would you like to change your style of goal-setting? If so, set definite goals for yourself and make plans to carry them through.

Ask the students in your class or group how they would like to develop goals.

CHANGES: PRESENT OR FUTURE?

Oftentimes educators speak about long-range and short-range goals, or comprehensive and specific goals. In the context of our considerations about conceiving learning as change and goals being the kinds of changes that are desired, we will consider

changes in the present (short-range, immediate goals) and
changes in the future (long-range comprehensive goals).

For your notes	*REFLECTION 6*
	1. What change do you think is most important for you to make at the present time?
	At this very moment?
	Within the next hour?
	Within the next day?
	Think!
	Think!
	Write and/or share!
	2. What change do you think is most important for you to make that you know cannot be achieved for a considerable period of time, and yet a decision must be made right now if you are to make these changes?

Think!
   Think!
      Write and/or share!
Now look at both of these desired changes. Do you see any relationship between them? Is one decision dependent upon the other?

We can approach this question about goals with two perspectives: in each case starting with one of the alternatives and following through to the other.

From the future to the present. (Long-range to short-range goals)

First, let us consider the need for beginning with the desired changes to be made in the future. There are situations where the future decisions determine our decisions in the here and now.

For instance, if there is a professional goal to be achieved in the future, a decision to strive for this profession imposes certain demands for changes that must be made now.

Or, suppose that a church sees the need to expand its educational facilities, some of the here-and-now decisions would have to point toward achieving the changes that will be taking place in the future.

Sometimes it is very necessary to make future decisions in order for our lives to have direction and meaning.

From the present to the future. (Immediate to comprehensive goals)

Now, let us consider beginning with the here-and-now decisions. These are the hardest decisions to make because we have to face ourselves realistically at the present time, saying,

      "This is what I must do now."

It is so much easier to think of what we might do in the future and talk about what we have done in the past. Although both of these are important, the here-and-now is determined by the past and will help in determining the future. We must be able to deal with the present if we are to deal with the future.

For example:

How do I feel about myself right now?

How do I relate to other people right now?

How is the Holy Spirit working in my life right now?

If we do not deal adequately with these questions right now, we are not able to plan for the future.

Present-future or future-present?

Can we make a value judgment as to which comes first: planning first for the changes in the present or in the future? We believe not.

The question is not an "either-or" situation, it is a "both-and" consideration. There are times when future plans take precedence over the here-and-now, but decisions made in the here-and-now may definitely affect or drastically change our long-range plans for desired changes. Let us suggest that it is a going back and forth from one to another in a state of fluidity that will keep us in balance and will keep us involved in a realistic and satisfying process of becoming.

Goals are thought of as desired changes to take place in persons — changes that need to be made if meaningful learning is to take place. Changes in knowing, feeling, and doing need to be planned. The teacher who can cooperatively plan with his students in setting goals for himself and his students will set conditions for the most effective learning to take place. Changes need to be planned for both the present and the future.

I WISH I COULD MAKE A LASTING IMPRESSION ON PEOPLE THE WAY YOU DO.

©1968 by United Feature Syndicate, Inc.

5
How Does Life-Style Effect Change?

Meet Mr. D

Mr. D is a person who is always seeking for new information. He understands himself and other persons. He is willing to share ideas with others and he listens to what others have to say. He risks himself in order to effect change. Mr. D has a positive life-style.

Meet Mr. E

Mr. E is afraid of change. He does not understand himself and there-fore he does not trust himself nor others. He finds it difficult to make decisions. He needs to control others in order to feel secure. He has a negative style of life.

Most people have certain ways of behaving. Each person has tendencies toward certain kinds of behaviors that are persistent and distinctive and make him a unique personality. We call this a style of life.

EXERCISE 18

Pretend that you are being interviewed by a news reporter who is to write an article about you in the daily newspaper. The column is to be entitled: "The Life-Style of . . . (add your name)." What information would you give to this reporter?

This chapter will assist you in defining your own life-style and help you analyze the life-style of other persons. Understanding a person's life-style will help us to determine what kind of a teacher and learner that person will be.

WHAT KINDS OF LIFE-STYLES?

Below are listed certain kinds of behaviors that people tend to exhibit.

In the left-hand column we list the kinds of behaviors that we label "positive" because they tend to make persons receptive to change when change is desirable.

(Mr. D is a person who is open to change.)

In the right-hand column we list the kinds of behaviors that we label "negative" because they tend to make persons resist change.

(Mr. E is a person who tends to resist change.)

Most persons have behaviors of both a positive and a negative nature but tend to have predominant behaviors in one of the areas.

In describing these two styles of life, we divide the characteristics into four areas of behaving:

— Knowing
— Feeling
— Doing
— Relational
(interpersonal)

For each behavior described we have the opposite behavior described in the opposite column.

POSITIVE LIFE-STYLE
(The life-style of Mr. D)

NEGATIVE LIFE-STYLE
(The life-style of Mr. E)

THE KNOWING AREA OF BEHAVING

POSITIVE LIFE-STYLE	NEGATIVE LIFE-STYLE
1. He is interested in problems and knowing how to solve them.	1. He is interested only in ideas.
2. He has convictions of his own.	2. He wants to be indoctrinated by others.
3. He is able to make decisions for himself.	3. He accepts decisions others make for him.
4. He asks questions to secure information and respects responses from others.	4. He desires one-way communication. He is threatened by dialogue.
5. He has personal insight.	5. He has few original ideas but often repeats what others say.
6. He evaluates information and accepts only what is valid for him.	6. He accumulates information without regard to its value.

Mr. D approaches life in a democratic and creative manner. He emphasizes the practical and existential approach to life. He does his own thinking and makes his own decisions and tends to be open to the possibility of change.

Mr. E approaches life in an authoritarian manner. He stresses the theoretical and the giving of information to others or accepting other people's opinions. He tends to manipulate persons. As a student he desires others to do the thinking. As a teacher he is in control. He tends to resist change.

EXERCISE 19

Evaluate yourself in regard to the six kinds of behavior listed above. Put a check mark in front of the qualities which you possess.

Do you tend to have a positive or negative life-style in the knowing area?

THE FEELING AREA OF BEHAVING

POSITIVE LIFE-STYLE	NEGATIVE LIFE-STYLE
1. He trusts himself and others.	1. He mistrusts himself and others.
2. He accepts other persons for what they are.	2. He judges other persons.
3. He appreciates what others do.	3. He criticizes other persons.
4. He is optimistic.	4. He is pessimistic.
5. He is brave.	5. He is fearful.
6. He is loving.	6. He is suspicious.

Mr. D is an authentic person who is secure enough to be free and open to change.

Mr. E tends to be an insecure person. Because he is fearful he is very rigid, restricted, and confined. He is afraid to face reality; so he is threatened by change.

THE DOING AREA OF BEHAVING

POSITIVE LIFE-STYLE	NEGATIVE LIFE-STYLE
1. He directly attacks a problem.	1. He retreats from facing a problem directly.
2. He becomes actively involved.	2. He is uninvolved.
3. He expresses his ideas through outward actions.	3. He expresses his ideas verbally in order to avoid action.
4. He is willing to risk.	4. He is afraid to risk, so he plays it safe.
5. He is spontaneous.	5. He delays action.

Mr. D sees things to be done and is willing to tackle them. He is disciplined by absorption in a task. He is willing to risk himself in order to achieve his goals.

Mr. E is passive and desires to keep the status quo. He is insecure and is afraid to risk.

THE RELATIONAL AREA OF BEHAVING

POSITIVE LIFE-STYLE	NEGATIVE LIFE-STYLE
1. He is honest with other persons.	1. He is afraid to be honest and open.
2. He is concerned with other persons.	2. He hides behind organizational structures for his security.
3. He is cooperative with others, having respect for others.	3. He isolates himself from others.
4. He gives of himself freely.	4. He is afraid to give of himself.
5. He is patient with others.	5. He is irritable with others who do not agree with him.
6. He is open.	6. He is defensive when attacked.

Mr. D relates well with other persons. He is concerned for them as persons of worth and identifies easily with them. He is a secure person and is willing to listen to what others are saying without being threatened.

Mr. E tends to be afraid of other persons. He usually displays defensive behavior in a group to protect himself because he is very insecure as a person.

A teacher's task is to develop his own life-style toward the possibilities of change and to assist others to do the same. Unless our life-style is predominantly positive, change will be negligible. Future chapters will further assist in analyzing ourselves and others in assisting persons to develop a life-style that is open to change.

A CHRISTIAN LIFE-STYLE

A person who has
identified himself with Jesus Christ, who has
dedicated himself to the Christian faith, and who
is allowing his life to be led by the Holy Spirit
HAS A CHRISTIAN STYLE OF LIFE

The spiritual aspects of living will permeate all of life, as Paul recorded:

I ask God, from the wealth of his glory, to give you power through his Spirit to be strong in your inner selves, and that Christ will make his home in your hearts, through faith. I pray that you may have your roots and foundations in love, and that you, together with all God's people, may have the power to understand how broad and long and high and deep is Christ's love. Yes, may you come to know his love—although it can never be fully known—and so be completely filled with the perfect fulness of God (Ephesians 3:16-19, TEV).

The Christian life-style is related to the four areas of life: knowing, feeling, doing, and relational.

The Knowing Area:

How great are God's riches! How deep are his wisdom and knowledge! Who can explain his decisions? Who can understand his ways? (Romans 11:33, TEV).

The Feeling Area:

The Spirit produces love, joy, peace, patience, kindness, goodness, faithfulness, humility, and self-control (Galatians 5:22-23, TEV).

The Activity Area:

"Do for others what you want them to do for you" (Matthew 7:12, TEV).

The Relational Area:

"You must love the Lord your God with all your heart, and with all your soul, and with all your mind. . . . You must love your neighbor as yourself" (Matthew 22:37-39, TEV).

We act and live as total human beings. In examining the Christian style of life, we note that the four areas relate to the positive areas of experience listed on the previous pages. (Go back to those pages and examine the relationships between the positive life-style and these characteristics of the Christian life-style.)

Our spiritual life reflects in our relationships, our pursuit of knowledge, our feelings, and our actions. On the other hand, the latter characteristics reflect the kind of spiritual life-style that we have. For example, a person who is very insecure will be a person with a mind closed to new truths. He will tend to become an extreme conservative or liberal. He has not allowed God to work in his life to give him freedom to live fully.

EXERCISE 20

Are you a person who is open to change, and therefore a teachable person? If so, write some goals that you would like to achieve.

Are you a person who is closed to change? If so, write some goals that will assist you in making yourself ready for change.

HOW DO LIFE-STYLES EFFECT CHANGE?

Being able to determine one's life-style will help a person know how he might assist others to change or how he might change himself. Not everyone changes in the same way. We start where people are and gradually open doors so that they may become freer to try new behaviors.

The secure person will be ready for direct confrontation of facts
and challenges to different ways of behaving. He is ready
for change.

(Mr. D is a secure person.)

The insecure person who has a poor concept of himself will
need indirect confrontation of new ways of behaving
coupled with a great deal of support. An authoritarian
person often is very insecure and therefore is afraid to
deal with emotions. He needs security and warmth as a
person before he can accept change and deal realistically
with his emotions and new ways of behaving.

(Mr. E is an insecure person.)

The passive person must be dealt with in a very warm and accepting manner. A person who is satisfied with the status
quo has a need for structure. His negative self-concept and
his tugging fears make him react negatively to a completely nonstructured experience. He needs some structure to feel comfortable. Later, when he gains self-confidence, he may be able to accept unstructured learning
experiences.

(Mr. E is a passive person.)

The compulsive person who has a deep compelling need for
change will welcome direct confrontation. He will be a
person of action, but may be concerned with change for
the sake of change. He needs assistance in seeing that
change is appropriate only when there is a purpose for it.

(Mr. D is a compulsive person.)

In general, persons whose behavior characteristics fall in the negative column need the loving care of concerned persons to open them up to the possibility of change
so they can be free
to live fully.
Life-styles may change or remain the same. Some life-styles

in themselves bring change. Life-styles can change, and we can be agents for them to change. The first step, however, is for us to be able to understand the life-styles of persons before we can know how to be a change agent. To analyze a person's life-style is not to judge that person, rather it is to understand him, and to accept him for who he is, and to assist him in the process of becoming a more effective person.

EXERCISE 21

How can you be an agent of change for specific persons in your group? What specific things can you do for each of these persons?

EXERCISE 22

How well do you know the persons in your group? Test yourself in a group session by playing the

GAME OF PERSONALITY

Ask each person in the group to finish the following sentence: "What would I do if (write in a problem situation) . . . ?" Ask each person to write three answers to the question, only one of which is correct.

Ask each member of the group, in turn, to give his three answers and let other members guess which response is correct.

How well do people know each other in your group?

SOMEHOW I JUST CAN'T SEEM TO GET ROLLING.

6
Why Do Persons Resist Change?

Over and over again we hear people say:

"Adults cannot change!"

"You can't change him!"

"He won't budge, no matter what you do!"

In response to the above statements we respond:

"We don't believe it."

We believe that adults can change. If we try to change a person, of course he won't change. Our first responsibility in knowing how a person can change is to know why some adults do not want to change now, or do not know how to change.

The most important thing is for the person himself to understand why he resists change. This is the first step in changing.

Let us examine some reasons why some adults resist change. Not all adults resist change for the same reason. We are arranging the reasons in seven categories: self-concept, fears, knowledge, moral standards, relationships with other persons, purposes, and the aging process. For each of these we will introduce you to at least one person who has a reason for resisting change.

EXERCISE 23

As you read about the various persons, see if you can identify yourself as similar to any of them. Are there some similarities to persons in your class or group?

AREAS RELATING TO THE SELF

EXERCISE 24

Look at yourself for five minutes in a mirror. While looking intently, ask yourself the questions:

—What is there about me that would make other persons like me?

—What is there about me that would make other persons dislike me?

Meet Mrs. F with her poor self-concept.

Mrs. F feels that she is not a person of worth. She says that other people have been telling her that all of her life. She has not been able to accept the fact that she was made in the image of God and that God loves her.

Mrs. F is unable to deal with her own limitations and does not recognize and accept her strengths.

When Mrs. F is in a group of people, she feels uncomfortable and insecure and is always conscious of what other people may be thinking of her. She will never make any contribution in a group because she is afraid of what other people will say.

Mrs. F is fearful of strong and overpowering personalities in a group. They are the kind of people who have always made her feel inadequate.

Mrs. F also has the feeling that as a woman she must be submissive. She has never been able to accept the role of a woman as a person of worth.

Meet Mrs. G with her excessive self-centeredness.

Mrs. G thinks only of herself and her own well-being. Her own self-worth is of utmost importance, and she uses it as an armor to protect herself from outside forces.

Mrs. G is too proud to admit at any time that she may be wrong. Instead, she crawls into a shell. She feels it is better to maintain her own integrity as an individual (as she thinks of it) than admit that she may be wrong. She thinks it is a weakness of character to admit any kind of failure or inadequacy.

Mrs. G is afraid of groups because she feels she may be pressured into becoming like other people in the group. She guards her own individuality with all her might.

FEARS

EXERCISE 25

Look in magazines and newspapers for pictures that represent fears that you and other people have. Completely cover a large piece of paper with these pictures.

Discuss these fears with the members of the group.

Meet Mr. H with his fear of failure.

Mr. H is filled with fears. Because society has built up in him the need for success, Mr. H is afraid of failure. He has not come to realize that failure of some kind is inevitable for everyone. Even Christ did not succeed in a human sense in many ways.

Mr. H is afraid to be ridiculed by others; so he remains silent in a group. If he remains silent, no one will know what he is thinking and that he is playing it safe. He does not want to be exposed.

Another reason why Mr. H is afraid to speak in a group is because he has difficulty in expressing his ideas clearly. If he makes a contribution, he fears that people may not understand what he is trying to say. He then becomes embarrassed and cannot clarify his meaning.

Meet Mr. J who feels that his integrity is threatened.

Mr. J also has many fears. He has a general fear of persons, especially ones who are more intelligent than he and those who are of a higher social standing. They are threats to his integrity.

Mr. J is afraid of change. Even the word "change" threatens him. He is satisfied with things as they are; so he is afraid to risk doing anything new.

Mr. J is afraid to take a stand on any issue because it will expose him as a person; so he hides behind other people's decisions. He cannot tolerate other people disagreeing with him; so he remains silent.

KNOWLEDGE

EXERCISE 26

Beside each of the fifteen words listed below write the first thought that comes to your mind when you see the word. Then put a plus or minus after the word or phrase, indicating whether your reaction to the word is positive or negative.

+ or —

feminine
masculine
manipulate
friendly
indulgent
dreamy-eyed
silence
change
black
white
red
aged
sympathy
easy
hard

Meet Miss K with her educational limitations.

Miss K has a limited educational background. Because of sickness she had difficulty completing high school. She seldom reads a book or a magazine and does not read the newspaper regularly. With her limited information, however, she has some very strong feelings about certain issues. She often secures information from unreliable sources that she has faith in, and therefore receives improper information about these issues.

Certain words are emotionally charged for Miss K. She does not always understand what they mean to other people nor does she want to. She has her own meanings and reacts to what persons say on the basis of these alone.

If a person uses a word that has negative connotations to her, she discredits everything else that this person says.

Miss K makes a lot of assumptions about people and things which sometimes are true and sometimes are false. She never checks, however, to see if the assumptions are right.

MORAL STANDARDS

EXERCISE 27

Write a statement, a litany, or a poem about how you feel about God at this very moment.

What words come to your mind as you think about God?

Meet Mr. L with strong feelings about his value system.

Mr. L has a value system that is his very own. His ways of believing, feeling, and doing are based upon these values. He has strong feelings about these values: they are his very being. When his values are threatened in any way, he feels threatened as a person and therefore resists change.

RELATIONSHIPS WITH OTHERS

EXERCISE 28

Look steadily into the eyes of another person for three minutes without glancing elsewhere. Try to look into the soul of the other person. What kind of a person do you think he is?

Talk about how you felt during this experience. What did you learn about yourself as well as the other person?

50

Meet Mrs. M with her preconceived ideas.

Mrs. M finds it difficult to relate to certain people. She has images of certain kinds of persons or groups of persons. For instance, Mrs. M has certain ideas about what a minister should be. She has certain expectations of a president of an organization. She regards any teacher with awe. She has not been able to consider persons filling these roles as individuals, but thinks of them as persons who are filling the kind of role that she expects them to play.

Mrs. M mistrusts persons who behave differently than she expects them to behave.

Mrs. M often makes preconceived judgments about persons without sufficient knowledge or reason. Her feelings are charged with deep emotional response, sometimes to the point of hostility.

Mrs. M finds it difficult to relate to people because she lacks the freedom to let herself go and to give herself to others.

EXERCISE 29

What images do you have of the following persons?
    minister
    housewife
    doctor
    female clergyman
    garbage man
    football coach
    waitress
    psychiatrist
Compare your images of these persons with those held by others.

Meet Miss N with her fear of controversy.

Miss N was recently elected president of the Women's Society of her local church. People expect her to carry on her work as president in the same way that previous presidents did. She would like to make some changes and do some things differently as a president, but she is afraid to even suggest these ideas lest people might not agree with them. Therefore, she keeps these feelings to herself and things go on as they always have.

PURPOSES

Meet Mr. O with his apathy.

Mr. O is apathetic to life in general. He is bored with life because he has no defined purpose in life to give him direction or cause him to be excited about anything.

Meet Mrs. P with her suspicion of new things.

Mrs. P is a member of a class with a new teacher. She expected that the new teacher would lecture all the time as the other teacher did. The new teacher, however, tried some new methods; but Mrs. P refused to respond. She mistrusted the purpose that the new teacher had for trying the new methods and cut herself off from any change.

THE AGING PROCESS

EXERCISE 30

Complete the following sentence:
   Aging is like . . .
Write as many similes as you wish.

Meet Mrs. Q in her isolation from continued
educational experience.

Mrs. Q is noticing the changes in her bodily functions as a result of the aging process. She no longer has the same amount of energy that she used to have, and her eyesight and hearing are not as keen as they used to be. When she was asked to become a member of a church school class, she refused. She had always thought that learning and church school were for children and youth and not for adults. Since she has been out of the habit of participating in any kind of an educational program for some years, the thought of becoming involved was terrifying to her.

The mere number of resistances stated in the illustrations in this chapter appalls us. It may even discourage us, but it need not.

Let us not say:
      "It seems impossible to overcome these barriers "
Let us attack it this way:
   Know the barriers;
      Understand them;
         Admit them; then
            Overcome them.

The next chapter will help us to see how these resistances may be overcome.

In looking at the illustrations in this chapter we note that the greatest number of resistances involve the feeling level of behaving. Our attitudes and our feelings primarily determine our will to change or not to change. Facts will be rejected, regardless of how right they may be, if our feelings toward ourselves, toward others, and toward God are not positive and growing.

A great many of the hindrances center around our self-concept and fears that are related to it. This insight gives us a clue to the secret of the possibility of change.

A happy outlook for the seemingly unhappy circumstances comes with the knowledge that some causes for resistance to change may also be potential causes for change, depending upon the intensity of the resistance and the circumstances in which the resistance occurs. Therefore, the inability to change may be only for the moment; the future may be brighter.

Before ecstasy
there must be agony.

7

When Do Persons Change?

Although adults may strongly resist change, we know that adults can change. A person working with adults must have this optimism. It is true that some adults change faster than others, but certain conditions will tend to produce a climate for change.

Before we discuss how adults learn or change, let us do some thinking about our own experiences of learning and try to analyze them.

For your notes	*REFLECTION 7*
	Recall situations in your life as an adult when you changed. (If you cannot think of any, turn to Reflection 8.)
	Recall one instance in each of the following categories:
	1. A time when you changed your mind. (Knowing)
	2. A time when you changed an attitude. (Feeling)
	3. A time when you changed your way of behaving. (Doing)
	In each of the above situations, answer the following questions:
	1. What influenced you to change?
	Was it a person, or a group of persons? If so, what kind of persons were they? What did they do to assist you in changing? Would you have changed if someone else had confronted you with the same influences?
	Did your relationship to God have a part in it? If so, how?
	What resources were used?
	Did it involve your will? If so, how?
	2. Under what circumstances did the

change take place? What was the setting? In what kind of room or place? Who was there at the time? What time of day was it?

3. What kinds of feelings did you have at the time? (anxious, cheerful, comfortable, elated, generous, hesitant, keyed-up, melancholy, obedient, peaceful, reckless, sad, self-assured, task-involving, trustful, vigorous, weary, worried, _____)

4. In what way did you change? In what ways were you a different person?

5. How has your life changed as a result of the experience?

(If you answered question 5, proceed to Exercise 31.)

For your notes

REFLECTION 8

Since you could not recall any experience of how you have changed, what does this say to you about yourself as a person?

I have a poor memory.

I am satisfied with the status quo: I am satisfied with things as they are.

I do not want to change.

I am always right.

I am playing God.

Other:

Answer these questions:

1. Do you feel that you are in the will of God? In what ways?

2. What kinds of feelings do you have about yourself? (Refer to point 3 in Reflection 7.) Compare the kinds of feelings that you have about yourself with persons who have said that they have changed. Are they the same in their feelings? Are they different? If so, in what ways?

(You may wish to go back to Reflection 7 and read the questions that are suggested. Then go to Exercise 31.)

EXERCISE 31

THE GAME OF IF

Round I—The realm of knowledge.

Reflect on an issue about which you have very strong convictions. Perhaps it is an issue on which you feel that you would never change your mind. Write the issue down so that you have it clearly in mind.

The Game of "If" is a game of pretending, so get ready to pretend. Do it by saying: "IF, IF, IF, (and only if) I were to change my mind on the issue about which I have strong convictions, what would have to happen to me as a person? What influences would be necessary for this change to take place?" (Record your answers on the Game Chart on page 58.)

1. What kind of person, or persons, would influence me? What kind of a person would I reject?

2. What kinds of information would I need to know?

3. What circumstances or conditions would have to exist? Would it have to take place in a certain location or building? Would I have to be alone, or with some other person(s)?

4. How would I need to be approached?

5. What kind of a mood would I have to be in?

6. What resources would I need?

7. What part would the Holy Spirit have to play? How would I know if it were the Holy Spirit guiding me?

8. What kind of a climate would be necessary (for example, accepting, forced)?

9. Would fear tactics help or hinder my decision?

10. What other factors would be involved?

Round II—The realm of feelings.

Reflect on a prejudice which you have about a certain person or a certain issue. If you feel that you do not have any prejudices, reflect on some issue or thing which you greatly dislike (for example, a color, a mood, a person, a kind of music).

Let us again pretend as we continue to play the Game of "If."

The rule of the game is to say: "IF (and only if) I were to change my feelings about this thing or person, what would have to happen to me as a person? How would I have to be influenced in order to change my mind?"

Answer the same questions as in the first round of the game and record your answers on the Game Chart.

Round III—The realm of doing.

Reflect on some act which you are doing with which you are greatly satisfied.

Let us again pretend as we continue to play the Game of "If."

The rule of the game is to say: "IF (and only if) I were to change my way of doing this act, what would have to happen to me as a person? How would I have to be influenced in order to change my way of doing this thing?"

Answer the same questions as in the first round of "If." Record your answers on the Game Chart.

After completing the three rounds, examine your chart. You have compiled some interesting information about yourself.

If we can understand what influences assist us in changing, it may help us in understanding how other persons change. Of course, we must realize that we do not all change in the same way.

The following influences tend to change persons.

1. A person.
2. A group of persons.
3. Acquiring information.
4. The use of resources.
5. An act of God: physical and/or spiritual.
6. Conditions conducive to learning.
7. The kind of approach made by people.
8. The kinds of feelings one has toward persons, situations, and self.
9. One's psychological makeup.
10. One's spiritual sensitivity.
11. One's sensitivity to persons.
12. The degree of trust one has in persons.
13. The degree of trust one has in himself.
14. The degree of trust one has in God.

Very seldom does only one phenomenon influence change. Almost always there is more than one kind of influence working simultaneously.

Meet Mr. R, a change agent.

Mr. R is seventy years of age and has been teaching a class of senior adults for many years. He finds it a real challenge. He knows that many adults resist change, but he is optimistic about adults learning because he himself has always found it a challenge to change. He realizes that some persons change more quickly than others. He has studied about how

GAME CHART FOR THE GAME OF *IF*

PERSONS	INFOR-MATION	CONDI-TIONS	AP-PROACH	MOOD	RE-SOURCES	HOLY SPIRIT	CLIMATE	FEAR TACTICS	OTHERS
ROUND I — The realm of knowledge.									
ROUND II — The realm of feelings.									
ROUND III — The realm of doing.									

adults change or learn; so he sets the kinds of conditions that allow persons to change if change is desirable. He understands when persons are ready to learn and the steps that they must take if they are to learn.

WHEN ARE PERSONS READY FOR CHANGE?

Persons change in different ways under different circumstances and for different reasons. Therefore, we cannot give an easy answer to the way anyone changes. We will consider various kinds of teachable moments and see how these can be used to effect change.

TEACHABLE MOMENTS

As with other age groups, adults will not learn until they are ready to learn, but when the time is ripe for change, we must be ready to take advantage of it. Teachable moments exist: (1) in time of conflict, (2) when there is a feeling of inadequacy, (3) when a need or problem is recognized, (4) when a goal is set, and (5) when a person is searching for meaning in life.

(Mr. R is always looking for teachable moments. Some are planned; others come spontaneously.)

TO CHANGE OR NOT TO CHANGE? — THAT IS THE QUESTION

Each teachable moment listed above presents possibilities for change but also presents the possibility for resistance to change. There is a period of suspension where alternatives are weighed. Which way the balance may tilt will depend upon certain circumstances and the kinds of persons who can assist. How the person will react will greatly depend upon his present life-style and way of behaving.

THE CROSSING POINT

If a person faces a situation which presents opportunities for change, then he must decide whether or not to change. What will determine his choice? This situation is the crucial moment that we must recognize and take advantage of.

This time of indecision is the ripe time for a crossing point to take place in a person's life. When a person is ready to learn, the gospel has something to say to him.

The person who senses this says:

"I need help!"

(Mr. R is sensitive to persons who are asking for help.)

The person who senses this says:

"I see you need help. Here is what the Christian faith says to you in this situation."

When the impact and thrust of the gospel brings about action in a time of crisis, there is a crossing point, for change has taken place in terms of the Christian faith.

The diagram below will further clarify this happening.

An issue is being faced　　　　The Christian faith speaks:

The teaching-learning situation
brings them together to produce

a crossing point

If we have a Christian style of life, each time of decision is a potential crossing point in our lives. When God's purposes meet mans' experiences, and responsive change takes place, a crossing point has occurred.

Let us now take each of the five teachable moments and see how they may be followed through steps that lead to change.

TEACHABLE MOMENT 1

In time of conflict. Conflict produces attraction toward and repulsion from a person or action. We must make a choice when we are confronted with conflict, and therefore there is a potential for change.

The alternatives

(When Mr. R sees a conflict, he realizes that there are two alternatives for the person to choose.)

The person may decide:
1. Not to change. He then exhibits some defensive behavior.
2. To change. He then is willing to confront the issue directly and be willing to resolve it.

Steps that will produce change

When there is a conflict of ideas	When there is a conflict of feelings	When there is a conflict in ways of acting
1. Reflect on issues.	1. Reduce negative feelings about the conflict.	1. Reflect on the present behavior.
2. Examine alternatives.	2. Examine alternative feelings.	2. Examine new ways of behaving.

3. Select new ways of thinking about the issues.	3. Select which feelings are acceptable.	3. Select an acceptable way of behaving.
4. Incorporate the new ideas into proper context.	4. Incorporate the new feelings.	4. Incorporate the new way into action.
5. Test for relevancy.	5. Test them out.	5. Test it out.

(Mr. R assists the person through the appropriate steps. He realizes that in each step there is a possibility of a potential crossing point.)

TEACHABLE MOMENT 2

A feeling of inadequacy. When a person feels that he has inadequate information or inappropriate feelings, or lacks skills, he may be ready for learning. When a person's present behavior does not receive confirmation from others, he may look for guidance for new behavior patterns.

The alternative

The person may decide:
1. Not to change. He then exhibits defensive behavior and has a feeling of despair.
2. To change. He will search for new information and new ways of behaving.

Steps that will produce change

When there is a feeling of inadequacy:

Of factual information	Of understanding	Of feelings	Of ways of behaving
1. Become aware of need for new information.	1. Become aware of need for new information.	1. Become anxious.	1. Become aware of need for new way of behaving.
2. Seek adequate resources.	2. Seek adequate resources.	2. Reduce or remove barriers to change.	2. Become aware of new ways of behaving.
3. Perceive new ideas.	3. Perceive new ideas.	3. Seek new ways of feeling.	3. Select a new way of behaving.
4. Imitate the idea of another.	4. Comprehend the meaning of the new idea.	4. Select appropriate new feeling.	4. Test the new behavior.

5. Repeat the idea until it is memorized.	5. Apply the new knowledge.	5. Incorporate the new feeling.	5. Get evidence of effectiveness of the new behavior.
6. Practice what has been learned.	6. Analyze situations involving the idea.	6. Test it out.	6. Use evidences to change self-perception.
7. Incorporate the new idea.	7. Synthesize into new patterns.		7. Incorporate new behavior into life-style.
8. Test it out.	8. Evaluate the new idea in relation to purposes.		8. See other uses for the new behavior.

TEACHABLE MOMENT 3

Recognition of a need or a problem. When a person faces a crisis in life, he is ready to seek help. He may not know where to find help or be willing to face the problem squarely, but there is potential for change, a readiness to learn.

The alternative

The person may decide:
1. Not to change. He then exhibits defensive behavior and has a feeling of despair. Apathy sets in.
2. To change. He defines the problem and directly confronts its solution.

Steps that will produce change

When there is a problem:

Relating to ideas and ways of acting	Relating to feelings
1. Define the problem.	1. Examine the feelings about the problem.
2. Gather relevant information about the problem.	2. Examine alternative ways of feeling about the problem.
3. Analyze the information gathered.	3. Select which feelings are appropriate and acceptable.
4. Determine alternative actions.	4. Incorporate new feelings.
5. Discuss solutions.	5. Test them out.
6. Select the most usable solution.	
7. Put the new solution into action.	
8. Test it out.	

TEACHABLE MOMENT 4

Setting a goal. When a goal is set, there must be means to reach it. Therefore, goal-setting is a potential learning situation.

The alternative

The person may decide:

1. Not to change. He then despairs because of inability to know how to meet the goal.
2. To change. He searches for ways to meet the goal.

Steps that will produce change

When the goal relates to:

Knowing and acting	Feeling
1. Clarify the goal.	1. Examine feelings relating to the goal.
2. Determine alternative ways of achieving the goal.	2. Examine alternative ways of feeling about the goal.
3. Select one alternative that is most viable.	3. Select which feelings are acceptable.
4. Incorporate the new ways of thinking and acting.	4. Incorporate the new feelings.
5. Compare the results with the goal.	5. Test them out.

TEACHABLE MOMENT 5

Searching for meaning in life. When a person is asking such questions as:

Who am I?
What has meaning?
What purpose exists for my life?
he is looking for answers.

The alternative

The person may decide:

1. Not to change. He is apathetic or despairs.
2. To change. He finds ways to make life meaningful.

Steps that will produce change

1. *Listening* with growing alertness to the gospel and *responding* in faith and love.

2. *Exploring* the whole field of relationships in the light of the gospel.

3. *Discovering* meaning and value in the field of relationships in the light of the gospel.

4. *Appropriating personally* the meaning and value discovered in the field of relationships in the light of the gospel.

5. *Assuming personal and social responsibility* in light of the gospel.[1]

We have seen that there are times when persons are more ready to change than at other times. We need to recognize the teachable moments which are: (1) times of conflict, (2) a feeling of inadequacy, (3) recognition of a need or a problem, (4) setting a goal, and (5) searching for meaning in life. Each teachable moment presents potential for change in the light of the gospel. Definite steps assist in the process of change. Each time of decision is a potential crossing point in our lives. When God's purposes meet man's experiences, change takes place.

In all the learning situations, the feeling aspect of learning is closely interrelated with the knowing and doing behaviors. In working with the patterns for change,

> *the feeling level must be dealt with before*
> *the other levels can be touched.*

Fundamentally, attitude change is necessary before change in actions or knowledge can take place. How useless is our teaching when we deal solely with facts or try to induce new actions but fail to deal with feelings and attitudes.

EXERCISE 32

Ask each person in the group to list as many feelings as he can think of in three minutes. Write these on paper. Ask each member to share his list, then discuss why each person listed the feelings that he did.

List all the feelings on the chalkboard or newsprint, tabulating the number of persons who listed each word. Discuss what this says about the members of the group.

Discuss how these feelings affect learning.

YOU GUYS JUST DON'T THINK *BIG* ENOUGH!

12-6 JACK WOHL
©1967 by United Feature Syndicate, Inc.

8
What Conditions Set a Climate for Change?

As we look into the settings in which adults change, we may begin by examining the ministry of Jesus. Jesus found himself in many settings, dealing with many kinds of persons under varying circumstances.

At times he felt the need to be

ALONE,

to pray and to meditate.

At other times he dealt with

ONE INDIVIDUAL,

meeting his individual need.

Often he met with

SMALL GROUPS OF PERSONS:

He gathered about him twelve men
who were his intimate companions.

We also see Jesus meeting with

LARGE CROWDS OF PERSONS.

Even in the large crowds he often
dealt with one individual or with
a small group of persons.

EXERCISE 33

Read through one of the Four Gospels and note the events in Christ's life. Record
   1. the number of times he was alone,
   2. the number of times he was with one person,
   3. the number of times he was with his disciples,
   4. the number of times he was with other small groups,
   5. the number of times he was with large crowds,
   6. the number of times he dealt with one individual or a small group while large crowds were around him.

In a study of Jesus' contacts with persons made by the author, a compilation of events recorded in the Four Gospels showed that of the 227 teaching situations of Jesus' ministry:

71 took place in large groups,
76 took place in small groups,

48 of which were with his twelve disciples,

17 took place with two individuals,

63 took place with one individual.

(Note: Sometimes it was necessary to make arbitrary decisions about the size of groups since insufficient information was given. We must also take into consideration that not all events of Christ's ministry were recorded.)

Change can take place in all of the following settings.

ALONE

Every person needs time alone. In silence,

he can contemplate,

he can meditate,

he can evaluate,

he can plan,

he can read,

he can pray.

ONE-TO-ONE ENCOUNTER

There is intimacy in conversing with one individual. This intimacy allows persons to be open and confiding, able to deal in depth with issues of common concern. Issues or problems that could not be exposed to large or small groups of persons can be confided to a person in whom we can have confidence and trust.

LARGE GROUPS

At times it is necessary for large groups of people to meet together. Information may be given by one person in a large group. There are many ways of involving persons in large groups, such as buzz groups, a reaction panel, or a workshop.

SMALL GROUPS

Much research has been done to show that much of the significant learning that takes place with adults is that which happens in small-group settings. Because such settings can offer a redemptive fellowship, we will concentrate on learning in the small-group setting.

WHY ARE SMALL GROUPS EFFECTIVE?

Persons need persons. When God made man, he stated that it was not good for him to be alone. We grow as persons as we relate to others. They contribute to our lives and we contribute to theirs.

We test our ideas with others.

We need confirmation from others.

Others help us become whole.

God is in the midst of "two or three."

We are confronted with ourselves as we are.

These experiences fill our need for belonging and fill our need for affection.

HOW CAN SMALL GROUPS BE EFFECTIVE?

The size of the groups must be small enough to allow for interactions among all persons who are meeting together. They need to be large enough to allow for sufficient differences of opinion to encourage interaction and to stimulate thinking.

The group needs to be small enough to allow all persons to contribute and to gain the most from the group. (Usually from eight to fifteen persons is the ideal size.) In an accepting atmosphere the small group provides the possibility for all group members to be treated as persons of worth.

WHAT PRINCIPLES OF GROUP WORK
EFFECT CHANGE?

The Christian faith is available at all times, but to be useful it must be encountered at strategic and teachable moments in a manner that will produce change. These conditions will be vehicles for the working of the Holy Spirit in the lives of persons.

A person must exercise his will if change is to take place. He must choose to be changed, but he must also know how to change. The principles of working with persons in groups will assist in this task.

Meet Mr. and Mrs. S

Mr. and Mrs. S are leaders of a small group of persons who gathered together for the purpose of exploring some of their common concerns. The group agreed to meet regularly for two hours each week and committed themselves to be present except for sickness. Each person in the group has a great deal of confidence and trust in Mr. and Mrs. S. As the individual persons had expressed their inadequacies to Mr. and Mrs. S, they agreed to join with others to learn how to change. Mr. and Mrs. S agreed to help them as they met together.

The group is composed of:

—Mrs. F, who has an inadequate self-concept;

—Mrs. G, who is self-centered and proud;

—Mr. H and Mr. J, who are filled with many fears;

—Miss K, who has a limited educational background;

—Mr. L, who has a value system about which he feels strongly and to which he clings tenaciously;

—Mrs. M, who finds it difficult to relate to people because of her preconceived ideas about their roles;
—Miss N, who is president of the Women's Society and fears controversy;
—Mr. O, who is apathetic to life in general;
—Mrs. P, who feels comfortable only with lecture because she is suspicious of new things;
—Mrs. Q, who has not been involved in any educational experience for many years.
(Refer to chapter 6 for more information about these persons.)
In working with these people Mr. and Mrs. S decided to use the following principles to assist the group members to change.

1. *Change takes place within a context of meaning.*

The learning experiences of adults need to be relevant to the needs of individuals. Since adults become involved in a teaching ⟷learning experience by choice, they can also discontinue their involvement if they so desire. The dropout rate in adult classes is alarmingly high. Adults desire information that can be put to use immediately.

When persons see meaning in what is presented, they are motivated to learn. Also, when persons are confronted with a problem, learning has meaning if it is presented in the context of solving the problem.

Any factual information is useless unless it is of value to the student and makes a difference in his life. Information is to be used to assist the individual to become more mature, not to enslave the individual with an accumulation of a great many unrelated, unmeaningful facts. What happens to the learner is the most important thing.

(Mr. and Mrs. S realize that each person in the group is looking for meaning in their lives.)

2. *Persons are more important than the information to be learned or the techniques used.*

All persons in a group should be treated as persons of worth. This can be done even if we do not agree with another person's ideas, or with his ways of feeling or behaving. We can recognize that this person has a reason for behaving the way he does. He may not be able to help himself and we do not help him by condemning him. He needs to be treated as a person with feelings that are rightfully his. Unproductive behavior often is a result of an inadequate self-concept. When we show our concern for the person, he gains confidence in himself as a person and therefore becomes more open for the possibility of change.

People must have faith in themselves if they are to function adequately. A person who does not have faith in himself cannot expect others to have faith in him. Persons, however, can assist others in gaining faith in themselves.

The more that we know of other persons the more we understand why they behave the way they do. When persons with divergent backgrounds and needs get together, their bases for communication are very minimal.

The accompanying Diagram I illustrates this point. A has something in common with B and different things in common with C. Likewise, B has things in common with A and C, and C has things in common with A and B. The area of experiences and understandings which all three have in common (note the darkened area) is very small. Also, a great many of the life experiences of each individual are known only to themselves.

The goal of the group experience is to expand the area of common experiences and understandings so that greater appreciation of the other person can take place. Diagram II shows this difference.

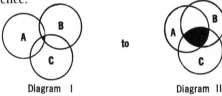

Diagram I   to   Diagram II

Addressing a person by name tells him that you know who he is and that you have regard for him as a person. Know each person in your group by name and use it occasionally when speaking directly to him.

(Mr. and Mrs. S realize how important each member of the group is. They are trying to develop this feeling among the other members in relation to each other.)

EXERCISE 34

In order for the leader to get better acquainted with the students he may ask them to complete the following sentences:
1. I am at my best when I . . .
2. I am at my worst when I . . .
3. I like people who . . .
4. I dislike people who . . .
5. I enjoy . . .
6. I detest . . .
7. I hope . . .
8. My next purchase will be . . .

3. *Significant learning takes place in an appropriate climate of interpersonal relationships between learners.*

When people accept others as persons, when there is empathy, and when people really listen to what other persons are saying, the climate is conducive to change.

In a supportive climate persons feel less need to defend themselves and their positions against attack. Behavior that is self-initiated occurs more readily in a climate that gives support. Persons develop and grow as autonomous persons with integrity. When they listen to each other, those persons who are speaking have opportunity to achieve a kind of purging of their emotions and feelings. This release is necessary for the reduction of the tensions that occur in all interpersonal relationships. When people feel comfortable and have support from others, they can perceive better. People who are accepted and understood by others tend to reach out to others in acceptance and empathy.[1]

A supporting climate is a caring climate, an open, free, non-judgmental atmosphere. Persons care for persons. People are not pressured into making decisions, and no one is always right. People are saying, "Lord, is it I?" rather than pointing a condemning finger at others.

A supporting climate is a patient climate. Persons who have developed long-standing habits or ways of thinking will not discard them immediately. It takes time to make new decisions which need to be made at a rate that is comfortable to the person. If force is imposed or pressure for a quick decision is applied, the change process may be disturbed and perhaps completely discontinued.

Faith and patience are partners. If we have faith in persons, we will also have the patience to wait until they are ready to take the step of change on their own initiative.

Informality often provides the climate for openness. An informal setting produces a relaxed atmosphere which is necessary for change. The group that restricts itself to following prescribed rules, especially those imposed upon them, tends to stifle creativity. Exceptions are in order, but calling people by their first names usually establishes a climate of friendliness. Informality in dress can also be a factor in assisting to break down barriers. Being dressed in "our Sunday best" may tend to inhibit freedom.

(Mr. and Mrs. S are aware of the need for a supporting climate among members of their group. Some members have a greater need for it than others.)

4. *Feelings are basic and prior to all learning.*

It is important for us to accept and understand our own and other persons' feelings. We must legitimize the existence and expression of feelings.

Without feelings we would be dead.

Without feelings we would be very uninteresting persons.

We should not be frightened by our feelings but understand them, even if they are negative. Understanding our feelings will be the first step toward the possibility of change.

A person must be accepted as a whole person. A person cannot be compartmentalized into cubbyholes of feelings, mental capacity, and behavior patterns. Every part of a person is affected by his entire being and we need to treat persons in relation to all of their capacities. Feelings, however, permeate our entire being and thus feelings are very important.

Facts are not accepted if feelings are intense about an issue. If feelings are riding high, people cannot deal with facts. Adequate information is needed but must be presented at appropriate times.

(Mr. and Mrs. S realize that they must begin working with the group first on the feeling level. The group is not yet ready to deal with deep, involved concepts.)

5. *The procedures to follow must be determined by the goals set by the learners.*

When the goals are determined by the learners, they are more ready to learn than when the goals are imposed upon them by the leader. Goal-setting should be a cooperative process if effective learning is to take place.

Goals need to be clearly defined so that all group members are clear about the direction in which they are going. When goals are not clearly defined, each individual has his own expectations and his own goals which bring chaos to the group.

Goals need to be defined in terms of desired behaviors. The behaviors should be those of knowing, feeling, and doing. Too often groups state goals that deal with knowing, and neglect the feeling and doing goals that are so essential.

EXERCISE 35

Ask the group to decide on an interest that is common to all. Then ask them to develop some goals related to this interest. Be sure to consider the knowing, feeling, and doing areas of concern. Refer to Chapter 4.

EXERCISE 36

Carefully look at the goal(s) prepared in Exercise 35. Examine the goal that deals with the doing aspect. Determine how the group can work together to achieve the goal so that change of action will take place.

Work together in small groups or have a brainstorming session. In a brainstorming session all suggestions are listed that are given by members of the group but without any comment or evaluation. After a designated time (perhaps ten minutes) the group discusses the pros and cons of the suggestions made.

A unity of purpose and respect for others in the group create cohesiveness. Persons then feel comfortable with each other and therefore are able to discuss problems openly without being threatened by other group members. Change takes place in a group that has cohesiveness because of a common purpose.

(Mr. and Mrs. S are working with the group to assist them to establish goals for themselves. This experience is new for the group and they find that it takes time for the members to get used to this procedure. They are patient with the members, however, and do not expect more from them than what they can handle.)

6. *Two-way communication sets a climate for change.*

Persons must be involved if they are to learn or to change. What the leader/teacher does is not as important as what happens to the group members/students. The task of the leader/teacher is to provide experiences in which each group member/student can be involved so that effective learning will take place.

The responsibility of the learning experience does not rest solely on the leader/teacher or a few individuals. Each person in the group must accept his responsibility to be an active listener, a ready participant, and a cooperative and helpful person to all learners, including the leader. Each person in the group must assume the responsibility of its success or failure.

A leader/teacher is a learner along with his group members/students and is not merely an imparter of information.

EXERCISE 37

Pose a problem to the group or have a member of the group propose a problem. Divide the entire group into triads (groups of three persons). Ask each triad to write a solution to the problem on a piece of newsprint which is then put on the wall with masking tape.

Ask each triad to move to the newsprint on their right and look carefully at the proposed solution before them. Give the groups three minutes to write their reactions below the proposed solution.

Again rotate the triads to the right and continue with the same procedure until each triad has had an opportunity to react to each solution.

Each triad then looks at the remarks written by the others to their proposed solution. After considering the other proposals, ask each group to come to a conclusion.

If desired, try to have the entire group come to an agreed solution.

Creative listening on the part of the leader and the group members is essential. Effective communication takes place only if persons are listening to each other. We listen because we have respect for others. We need to listen to what the other person is saying and then restate what we think we heard to be sure that we have a meeting of meanings.

EXERCISE 38

During a period of discussion, each person is asked to restate what he thinks the previous person has said before he makes a contribution. This exercise forces each person to listen carefully and gives him an opportunity to check whether or not he understands what others are saying.

If we are good listeners, we are not afraid of silence. Many times we feel that if no one is saying anything, nothing is happening. On the contrary, more might happen if there would be more silences in our meetings. We need time to think through alternatives. When a question is asked, we need time to think. We would be less embarrassed if we make statements that are thought through carefully. Then we would avoid giving quick answers that may be embarrassing and hard to retract. Silent moments can also be moments in God's presence, asking for divine wisdom and strength to open ourselves to others.

As we share ideas and react to other persons' ideas, we need to be sensitive to persons and to consider how they will react to what we say. Sensitivity needs to be developed to the kinds of tonal qualities which evoke a positive reaction. Words spoken harshly with high emotional intensity very often are rejected by the person to whom they are spoken.

A word with a sting
May not mean a thing
  To an insecure person.
A word with a bite
May be just right
  For a secure person.
It is not what you say,
  But how you say it,
  To whom you say it, and
  The time that it is said
That makes the difference.

EXERCISE 39

Say the following phrases in at least three different tones:
1. Why did you do that?
2. I don't know how to react to that remark.
3. Will you say that again, please?

How do you think persons would react to each tone?

Think of specific persons whom you know who would react in a positive or negative way to the different tonal qualities.

An atmosphere of trust, security, and mutual confidence must exist so that each member feels free to express his ideas honestly. Each member must learn to accept help when given and to react positively to those who are sensitive to his needs.

Faith in oneself, faith in other people, and faith in God are necessary for an interactive redemptive fellowship.

(Mr. and Mrs. S know that they are not to be leaders in the traditional sense. They are to interact with the persons in the group until there is a meeting of meaning. The fact that Mr. and Mrs. S are trusted and respected by the members of the group will help this interactive process. The persons in the group, however, must have trust in each other before the interactive process can be effective.)

EXERCISE 40

In order to develop the kind of trust which assures a person that he is being heard, this exercise may be used.

Divide the group into triads (three persons). In each triad, one person will be the speaker, one person the listener, and one person the observer.

Designate a portion of the Bible or another book to be read by all members. Ask the "speaker" in each group to report what he thinks the author is saying. Ask the "listener" in each

74

group to listen carefully to the "speaker." Ask him occasionally to repeat what he thinks the "speaker" has been saying and continue to clarify until there is agreement about meanings. The "observer" in the group is to be silent and observe what is going on between the other two persons. When the "speaker" and "listener" have reached agreement, the "observer" reports on whether or not an atmosphere of trust is present.

Continue this procedure for two additional times, rotating roles so that each person will have an opportunity to be a speaker, a listener, and an observer. Then the group should discuss what they have learned about two-way communication.

7. *Nonverbal communication is as important as verbal communication.*

Persons sometimes say more in their actions than they say in their words. Communication is often portrayed by the following:

Posture
Facial movements or lack of them
Body-twitching
Hand movements

Foot movements
Eye contact or lack of it
Retreat from the circle
The tilt of the head

Some movements may be due to physical deformities or deficiencies or discomfort at the moment and not to emotional inadequacies. We must learn to sense the difference or check with the persons about the situation. We might ask:

"Frank, do you think we need more air in the room?"

"Joyce, are we speaking loudly enough?"

Other movements, however, may express the emotional reactions of the group members.

EXERCISE 41

Watch the physical movements of a person. Select one part of the body and concentrate on that. Watch the movements and describe them, then write what you think the person might be saying by these movements. List as many ideas as you can.

If you think the person can accept it, confront him with your observations and let him tell you what they meant. Tell him what you thought he was saying. Talk about the implications of these observations.

What did you learn about the person?

What did you learn about yourself?

What did you learn about nonverbal communication?

There are ways that a leader may communicate nonverbally with members of the group. There may be eye contact, a nod of the head, a smile, or even a frown that conveys meanings to individuals. These same methods take place between members of the group and are important to observe.

EXERCISE 42

Ask the group members to be silent for five minutes. Request that they communicate nonverbally in as many ways as they wish with others in the group.

After the five minutes, request members of the group to see if they communicated what they thought they were communicating.

(Mr. and Mrs. S are constantly aware of the nonverbal communication that is taking place in the group.)

8. *Interpersonal relationships between the learner and the leader must progress from the supportive climate to the direct challenge.*

The adult brings many experiences with him to a teaching←→ learning situation. He has knowledge, deep-seated feelings, prejudices, and preconceived ideas. The leader must accept the adult as a person of worth with all of these conditions, first giving him support and then assisting him progressively to accept himself, to understand why he behaves as he does, and then to face a direct challenge of his beliefs. An abrupt challenge to an insecure adult may retard learning or spoil all opportunities for learning to take place.

Change does not take place without conflict. God has made man so that he must make choices. Choices help a person to grow. If there were no frustrations and no conflict, no one would change. Bridges are built upon tension and stress. Snyder has said that perhaps persons are significantly alive only in moments of choice and decision.[2]

To be maturing persons, we must develop a tolerance for frustration. This can only be done with

> an adequate self-concept,
> a security as a person,
> a concern for others, and
> a deep faith in God
>> which brings
>> purpose to life.

Some persons, however, are not ready for conflict and react

to it negatively rather than being willing to face it. We need to learn to recognize those persons "who can take it." We must also be sensitive to those who need support. To these we must give support until they are ready to risk themselves in conflict. A caring ministry involves knowing when people are ready to risk. Paul told Timothy

"to convince,
reproach,
and encourage,
teaching with all patience"
(2 Timothy 4:2*b*, TEV).

The following diagram may assist you in determining your responses to persons.

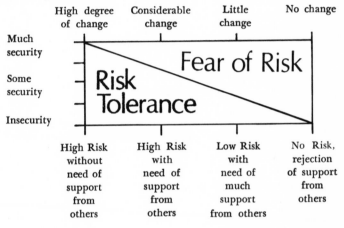

Qualities of risk-taking person.

1. Strong
2. Adequate and realistic self-concept
3. Great tolerance for frustration
4. Openness
5. Free from concern about reaction from others
6. Free to experiment
7. Free in Christ

Qualities of risk-fearing person.

1. Weak
2. Inadequate and unrealistic self-concept
3. No tolerance of frustration
4. Protective wall
5. Great concern about reaction from others
6. Fight for one's own survival
7. Bondage to tradition

When a group of persons come together for the first time, there is usually need for supporting persons. As they get to know each other and understand each other, trust develops. Sensitivity needs to be developed to know which persons fear risking and which ones have a great tolerance for risking. In a supporting climate of acceptance, persons develop a tolerance for risking.

To show the reason for moving from a supportive climate to a direct challenge, Anderson shows how persons change in a group. There is a movement:

1. From self-centeredness to care for others.
2. From doubt about self to trust of self.
3. From irresponsibility to a sense of responsibility for self and others.
4. From secrecy to sharing.
5. From unfreedom to freedom.
6. From mistrust to trust.
7. From the need to receive ministry to a concern to give ministry.
8. From a closed mind to a mind open to learning.
9. From fear of self, neighbor, and God to love of self, neighbor, and God.[3]

As persons move in these ways, there will be more risking, more change, and more learning taking place.

EXERCISE 43

Line from eight to twelve chairs in a row, depending upon the number of persons in the group. (The number of chairs can be the same as, or less than, the number of persons in the group.)

Indicate the chair at the one end of the row as representing "trust" and the chair at the opposite end as representing "no trust." The chairs in between represent progressively smaller degrees of trust.

Ask either of the following questions and have each student choose the chair which represents his answer:

How much trust do I think that people in the group have for me?

or:

How much trust do I have in the members of the group as a whole?

If necessary, ask students to stand in **back** of the appropriate chair if someone has already sat in the one which he has chosen.

Talk about your feelings of trust. Why is trust evident? Why is there mistrust? How can trust be developed?

9. *Evaluation should be a constant process in the teaching* ⟷ *learning situation.*

We usually think of evaluation as a process that takes place at the end of a teaching←→learning situation. Constant evaluation, however, is necessary to determine whether or not progress is being made toward achieving the goals which have been set. At appropriate times it is well to pause in the teaching←→learning situation to evaluate consciously the kind of progress which has been made and, if necessary, to change the plan of procedure toward achieving the goals. An evaluative climate in a teaching ←→learning situation brings about significant learning.

EXERCISE 44

Place the chairs in the room in two concentric circles with the same number of chairs in each circle. The persons sitting in the inside circle will carry on the discussion of the topic at hand and the persons in the outside circle will evaluate the interaction of persons who are discussing the topic. Ask the observers to look for the following factors:
1. Is the atmosphere tense or relaxed? Why?
2. How does the leader affect the members of the group?
3. How do the members of the group affect the leader?
4. Do persons support other persons' contributions?
5. Are persons listening to each other?
6. Are persons looking at each other?

After the discussion ask the members in the outer circle to report their findings. Request the observers to describe what they saw rather than criticize behavior. Unless the group is very cohesive, it would be well not to use names when reporting.

Since evaluation of a person may be threatening to him, it is important to evaluate in a nonthreatening manner. A person usually resists change when he is attacked as a person. His own integrity is questioned; so he rebels. When a person's behavior is questionable, it is more helpful to attack what he has done rather than to attack the person himself. Descriptive statements of behavior will not be likely to arouse hostility. For example, consider the problem of a person who always comes late to a meeting. If someone makes the statement "You're late again! Why can't you be on time?" the person is threatened. But if someone says something like this: "Tardiness delays effective working of our group. If all members come on time, we can get through with our meeting earlier and all of us will have a good feeling." This kind of evaluation describes the situation but does not directly attack the person.

Write the following judgmental statements in descriptive terms:
1. What! You didn't read your lesson again?
2. I can't understand why you always have to bring up the same issue! We've gone over this matter hundreds of times, but you don't seem to listen.

10. *Physical conditions and arrangements hinder or help learning.*

The amount of space, seating arrangement, temperature, ventilation, lighting, location of the room, and a person's physical well-being definitely affect learning.

Too many persons in a room may cause discomfort and fears on the part of some adults. One's own physical well-being takes precedence over any learning that might take place. *Have adequate space: at least ten square feet per person.*

Chairs lined in a row so that persons see only the face of the teacher/leader do not allow for effective interaction between other persons in the group. *Chairs should be arranged in a circle for eye-to-eye contact.*

Room temperature that is too warm or too cold may cause discomfort that makes learning impossible. *Temperature between 70 and 72 degrees usually is comfortable for learning.* A higher temperature is sometimes necessary for older adults.

Too little or too much ventilation may cause mental inactivity. *Try to provide good circulation of air.*

Poor lighting creates a gloomy atmosphere and also does not allow persons to read or see any visual presentation that is made. *Make sure of adequate lighting.*

Adults whose hearing is somewhat impaired have special needs. *The room should be located where few noises from the outside are heard. The group should be small so that all can hear well.*

Physical well-being is necessary for change. A person whose physical condition is not up to par has greater difficulty in dealing with change than other persons.

It is possible for adults to change. The process of changing is easier for some than for others. Ten principles assist the process of change:
1. Learning experiences need to be relevant.
2. Persons are more important than information.
3. An appropriate climate of interpersonal relationships is necessary.

4. Definite goals need to be set by the learners.
5. Feelings are prior and basic to all learning.
6. Two-way communication is necessary.
7. Nonverbal communication is important.
8. A progression from a supportive to a direct challenge encourages change.
9. Evaluation must be a constant process.
10. Physical conditions and arrangements hinder or help communication.

Risk is always involved when we decide to change and also when we assist others to change, but through risking we become creative and useful persons. Risking also involves the possibility of failure, but unless we risk we never grow. Failure is not always bad. Jesus' crucifixion, thought by many to be his downfall, resulted in later resurrection and in victory.

Risking may result in a resurrected life.

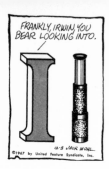

FRANKLY, IRWIN, YOU BEAR LOOKING INTO.

©1967 by United Feature Syndicate, Inc.

9
What Techniques
Effect Change?
Part I

A creative person
can find many ways
to assist persons to change
if he really wants to, and
if he is willing to risk.

TO LECTURE OR NOT TO LECTURE?
— THAT IS THE QUESTION

At times lectures are very appropriate and the best teaching method for the teacher and class. Most teachers of adults, however, use lecture as the main or only form of teaching. We, therefore need to understand the importance of this rule:

Never,

    Never,

        Never lecture,
        unless there is
        no other way
    to help persons learn.

Search,

    Search,

        Search
      for other ways first,
        then,
        if there is
      no other way,
    the lecture
    is for you.

There are some valid reasons for suggesting this rule. Let us look at them.

First: The lecture is the *easiest* way for the teacher, *but* the *most difficult* one for the student. The entire learning process is dependent upon the student.

Second: The lecture is the *safest* way for the teacher. It has no threat for him; there is no opportunity for students to challenge. *But* it is the *dreariest* way for the student.

Third: The lecture is the *quickest* way for the teacher *but* the *least interesting* way for the student.

Fourth: The lecture makes the *teacher* the most important person, *not* the *student*.

When Kallen talks about the lecture, he has this to say:

> This teacher-pupil relation is particularly apt for authoritarian personalities among teachers. It is their vehicle of self-expression. And it is apt for submissive, masochistic personalities among pupils, whom it somehow frees from feelings of anxiety about their present condition and future fortunes. Not a few adults seeking education come questing for this liberation. But rather regularly, when the teacher-pupil relation is such, teaching tends to become the prime barrier to learning. The pupil does of course learn, but he learns the teacher, and the subject only in so far as it is a function or appanage of the teacher's personality.[1]

Many teachers would claim:

"But students want me to lecture."

"Students don't want to participate."

"Students won't discuss. I ask a question and they just sit there!"

Have you ever thought why teachers say these things? As a teacher, have you perhaps made a similar retort?

For your notes	REFLECTION 9
	Why do you lecture? Be honest with yourself. Ask yourself these questions:
	1. Am I afraid to use other methods?
	2. Do I trust other persons?
	3. Do I trust myself?
	4. Am I afraid to risk?

Think about these conditions in relation to the reasons you gave for lecturing.

— Students may not know any other way of learning.

— Students may want to participate but don't know how to, or the climate in the group may not be right for good participation.

— If students won't discuss, you haven't asked the right questions.

Through the lecture method students really are not learning as much as you think they are. Their failure to learn may become evident in the lack of any real change in their lives. One very vivid demonstration of the short-comings of the lecture method is the domino experiment described in Exercise 46. Try it with your group and see for yourself.

EXERCISE 46

Round 1.

Request one person from the group to take four dominoes and stand somewhere in the room where no one can see him work. Request him to set the dominoes in any position he desires, then ask him to describe how they are placed. Give the other members of the group four dominoes each, or give them a piece of paper and pencil. Then ask them to carry out the following rules:

1. Place, or draw, the dominoes in the positions that are described.

2. Make no comments, no reactions, or ask no questions of the person speaking.

3. After each person has placed, or drawn, the dominoes, request the person speaking to show how he placed his dominoes and have others compare theirs.

Now record the following items:

1. The number of persons who placed the dominoes correctly. (The position must be exact.)

2. The number who failed.

3. The time it took.

Round 2.

Request the same, or another, person to go to a place in the room that is not observable to the others and place the dominoes in any position desired. Request that he describe how the dominoes are placed.

The rules for the other members of the group are as follows:

1. Place, or draw, the dominoes in the positions that are described.

2. Ask any questions of the speaker that you desire in order to clarify what has been said.

3. Rearrange your dominoes until you are satisfied that they are placed as described.

When all persons have asked as many questions as they desire, compare the placement of the dominoes with the original, and record the three items listed above: correct placement, incorrect placement, and time. Then compare these three results with the findings for the first round.

What does this have to say to you about communication?
What does this say to you about the lecture?

When you must use the lecture, use other resources with it:

> the chalkboard or newsprint;
>
> an overhead projector;
>
> an opaque projector;
>
> maps;
>
> pictures;
>
> charts;
>
> illustrative objects.

Lecture for only brief periods of time and intersperse the lectures with other techniques.

Have you ever thought of tape-recording your lecture? Those persons who want to listen to a lecture can listen to the tape and you can spend time with those who are interested in becoming involved in other educational experiences.

LEARNING CAN BE FUN

When having fun we:

> — have some tensions
>
> — are involved in some process
>
> — have satisfaction of some need
>
> — have enjoyment in the process.

All of these elements are involved in a profitable teaching↔ learning experience.

Few people believe that learning can be fun because they have never experienced it in this way. The following seventy techniques, described in this chapter and the next, will show that learning can be a pleasurable experience.

> Caution: Techniques are not ends in themselves. They are only valuable in relation to the purpose (s) which they are designed to achieve. We should ask ourselves the questions:
>
> 1. What kind (s) of change do we want to take place?
>
> 2. What technique (s) will best assist in bringing about this change?

These techniques are listed in relation to goals or the kinds of changes desired. Techniques should be chosen in accord with the goals, purposes, or needs of the group (A and B in this chapter, C through H in the next chapter).

A. To gain information (sixteen ways).

B. To contribute and gain opinions about an issue (eighteen ways).

C. To secure solutions to a problem (eight ways).

D. To have firsthand experiences (four ways).

E. To encounter biblical truths (eight ways).

F. To express oneself in creative ways (twelve ways).

G. To reflect on inner feelings (two ways).

H. To accomplish a task (two ways).

Under each of the above goals will be listed techniques to assist you in bringing about changes in yourself and other persons.

A. Desired change: TO GAIN INFORMATION.

1. *Book Report.** Summarize and interpret the thoughts of an author. Present key ideas in an interesting manner. When appropriate, tell the key ideas by presenting the information in the first person. (Techniques marked with an * are described in greater detail in the author's book, *40 Ways to Teach in Groups,* published by Judson Press, 1967.)

2. *Colloquy.** Three or four persons selected from a group present various aspects of a problem to three or four resource persons who respond to them. If desired, the entire group can be divided into smaller groups of five or six persons. Each group lists some questions which they would like the resource persons to answer. Select one person from each group to serve on a panel to ask the questions posed by the group.

3. *Group Response Team.** When a lecture is given by the leader or by an invited guest, select a few persons from the audience to sit in front with the speaker. As the speaker gives the lecture, the selected persons interrupt at any time that they do not understand or agree with the lecturer.

4. *Interview Forum.** A guest is invited to the group. The leader asks the guest questions about a topic of interest to the group. After the conversation between the two persons, opportunity is given to all members of the group to participate.

5. *Lecture.** The presentation of information in a formal speech, sometimes accompanied by visual materials.

6. *Lecture Forum.** A speech is followed by a free and open discussion of the topic by all members of the group.

7. *Panel.* Several persons are asked in advance to read about a specific topic. They gather around a table in the front of the room where the leader asks them appropriate questions about the topic. The members respond spontaneously and also talk among themselves about the issues involved. (Note: This is often confused with the symposium which is described in Item 14. Please note the difference.)

8. *Programmed Materials.* For individual study, books which are "programmed" with responses for the student are very helpful, especially for content-centered materials. These books have brief explanations of principles, followed by questions or illustrations of problems that relate to the principles. The correct answers are given so that students can study by themselves. (See *This Covenant People,* by Harold Malmborg, George W. Peck, and Edwin F. Taylor, published by Judson Press, 1970, for an example of programmed Bible study.) Some programmed materials are prepared with alternative designs so that those with more advanced knowledge may advance more rapidly through the book by skipping some of the elementary concepts.

9. *Questions and Answers.** The teacher asks questions to which he desires a direct response, or students ask questions of the teacher. (Note: This technique differs from group discussion, where all persons are expected to respond to the question at hand.)

10. *Reaction Panel.** After a speech, film, or symposium a few persons from the audience are requested to come to the front of the room where they join the leader and/or other persons. Together these persons react to what has been said and/or seen. They carry on a discussion before the audience. (Note: This technique is primarily designed for large audiences, since smaller groups can carry on the discussion among all members of the group.)

11. *Research and Report.** Individual students volunteer or are requested to do some research on a problem of interest to them and to the entire group. The research is done outside of the class and the results brought to the class at its next session. Students react to the report of the research to clarify meanings and perhaps to determine other areas of the subject that need to be explored.

12. *Screened Speech.** A general topic is selected, and then small groups are formed to determine specific questions which they would like to have answered about this topic. These questions are recorded on slips of paper which are given to a speaker. A speech follows that seeks to answer the questions presented by all the small groups.

13. *Seminar.** A small group of persons meets regularly to present research studies which individuals have prepared. The areas of research are determined by the individuals and reported to the group. After each research study is presented to the entire group, the individuals in the group react to the material

presented, discussing its meaning and determining its implications for their lives.

14. *Symposium.** Several persons are selected from the group, or several guests are invited to the group. A topic is selected for consideration and then divided into subtopics. Each subtopic is given to one of the selected persons. Each person prepares a brief speech on his subtopic and presents it to the group.

15. *Symposium Dialogue.** After the series of short speeches are presented in the symposium technique, described above, an expert in the field is requested to react to the speeches. He presents both support and challenge, and asks questions for clarification. He also adds further information on the general topic that was not covered by the symposium members.

16. *Time Line.* Whenever a series of historical events is studied, a time line assists in understanding relationships between events. The line can be made in several ways. A piece of heavy string can be attached to two surfaces in the room so that the string itself becomes the time line. Or, a long piece of shelf paper can be attached to the wall of the room. Then the time line is a line drawn across the middle of the paper from one edge to the other. Now, divide the line into periods of time, such as months, or years. When time periods are not clearly designated, the time line can be used for indicating the sequence of events rather than exact time periods. Essential information about appropriate events can be written on baggage tags which can be tied to the string, or can be written on the paper along the time line. Pictures of personalities involved in the events can also be added. The use of pictures and various colors of pens can make the time line more attractive and more valuable as a learning tool.

B. Desired change: TO CONTRIBUTE AND GAIN OPINIONS ABOUT AN ISSUE.

1. *Cinema Talk-Back.* The group can attend a cinema and then talk about the issues that were implicit in the film. The following questions might be asked:

a. What was the main theme of the film?
b. What kinds of relationships were shown?
c. In what ways were persons helping each other?
d. In what ways were persons hurting each other?
e. What kinds of changes took place in persons? How and why did they take place?
f. What does this film say to me as a person?

2. *Circle Response.** When there is a small group of persons and a desire to have everyone respond to an issue, the circle response provides for this. When a question is asked or a problem posed, each person in turn is asked to respond to the question. No one is allowed to speak a second time until each person has had an opportunity to speak once.

3. *Debate Forum.** Two teams of at least two persons each are requested to take opposing views on an issue. The speakers who are "for" the issue present their views and are then followed by the speakers who are "against" the issue. A brief time of rebuttal is allowed for each person, speaking in the same order as the first speeches were made. After the presentation of the debate teams, the matter is discussed by the entire group. The debaters should be included in this discussion time.

4. *Expanding Panel.** Several persons are seated in the center of the room as a panel. The other persons are seated in a circle surrounding them. The panel members discuss a topic that has been assigned to them. They do not present speeches but respond to issues that are raised within the panel. After discussing the issue for a period of time, they move their chairs back into the circle and all members of the group participate in the discussion.

5. *Film Talk-Back.** A film is introduced to the group by means of a few remarks about its purpose and theme. After the film is shown, the members of the group discuss the message of the film and its relationship to their lives. (Note: The questions posed in the Cinema Talk-Back are also applicable here.)

6. *Floor Montage.* The leader displays a group of magazine covers and newspapers on the floor in the middle of the circle of chairs. The items can be overlapped and arranged in an attractive array, such as a circular arrangement. If desired, the members of the group can be asked to bring magazines and newspapers and help arrange the display. Since the items displayed on the floor represent issues of the day, the discussion of the group can center around the issues that are expressed in pictorial form. The great variety of issues in itself can be an item for discussion.

7. *Gallery Conversations.** Several paintings or pieces of sculpture are displayed before the group. Group members try to search for meaning in the artistic works. Such questions as the following might be asked:

a. What do you think the artist is trying to convey?

b. What meaning does the piece of art have for you? (Note:

For example, display different pictures of the head of Christ and discuss how the artists have portrayed different characteristics of Christ's personality through these paintings.)

8. *Group Discussion.** The group discusses a topic of mutual interest. All members of the group have responsibility for the success of the learning experience. All listen carefully to what other persons are saying, build upon the contributions of others, and freely and openly express opinions. Balanced participation by all members is sought.

9. *Group Drawing.** The group is divided into subgroups. Each group decides on some common ideas about an assigned topic. One person in each group is asked to put these ideas into some pictorial form. Later the drawings are shared by the entire group and discussed. Some groups may wish to have all members of their subgroup participate in the drawings.

10. *Group Sculpturing.* The group is divided into subgroups of three or four persons each. Each subgroup is given a large piece of clay and asked to form it into some symbolic form. All members of the group are to assist in producing the form. This experience should be carried on without saying any words. After a designated time the sculptures are shared with other groups. Persons discuss the meanings of the sculptured forms. They also share their feelings as they worked together as a group.

11. *Group Writing.** The group is divided into subgroups. Each subgroup decides on some common ideas about an assigned topic. Each smaller group engages in some form of creative writing to express these ideas. The writing may take the form of a litany, poem, prayer, story, news item, or any other form desired. After a designated time each subgroup shares their contributions with the other groups.

12. *Listening Teams.** This technique is always combined with another technique, such as a lecture, film, or a symposium. Before the other technique is presented, the leader divides the group into several subgroups. Each subgroup is given one or more questions to consider while the presentation is made. Each subgroup is given a different set of questions. After the presentation, each subgroup presents their reactions to the entire group, and a general discussion ensues.

13. *Music Forum.** The group listens to some kind of music and reacts to it. They consider the kind of mood the music creates. If there is a lyric to the song, they discuss its meaning. They then consider what meanings this musical composition

suggests which have some relationship to their life situation.

14. *Novel Talk-Back.* The group reads a novel and discusses its meaning for them. The novel may be one of the best-seller books or may be a biblical novel. The experiences in the novel are discussed in detail with the intent of determining the meanings intended by the author. (Note: The same questions presented in the Cinema Talk-Back would be appropriate.)

15. *Panel Forum.** Several persons discuss a topic before a group. After this presentation, all members of the group participate in discussing the topic presented.

16. *Sermon Forum.** After a sermon is given, members of the audience are given an opportunity to respond to it. The entire congregation may discuss the problems suggested in the sermon, or subgroups can be formed. The subgroups can prepare questions to be asked of the speaker at the end of a designated time.

17. *Symposium Forum.** Three or four speakers give brief presentations of various subtopics of an issue. Their presentations are followed by free and open discussion of the topic by the members of the group.

18. *Television Talk-Back.* Members of a group watch a television program and discuss its significance to them. (Note: The same questions asked in the Cinema Talk-Back would be appropriate in some cases.)

10
What Techniques Effect Change? Part II

In the previous chapter several techniques were listed which are valuable in relation to the goals of gaining information, and contributing and gaining opinions about an issue.

Now we continue to consider techniques for bringing about other kinds of changes. (As in the previous chapter, techniques marked with an * are described in greater detail in *40 Ways to Teach in Groups*.)

C. Desired change: TO SECURE SOLUTIONS TO A PROBLEM.

1. *Brainstorming.** A problem is posed to the group. One or two persons are selected as recorders. Members of the group are asked to give proposed solutions to the problems in rapid succession. These solutions are recorded on the chalkboard or on a piece of newsprint. If two recorders are used, they may take turns in recording the solutions. No comments are to be made regarding the proposed solutions as they are being given. After a designated time, the group members evaluate the solutions, eliminating those that are not practical. Sometimes a small group may be selected to do the evaluation and report to the entire group at a later date.

2. *Buzz Groups.** The large group is divided into subgroups of from four to six persons each. A problem is posed and each subgroup deals with the problem, offering solutions. One person in each group is selected as leader, and one as recorder. After a designated time, the recorder from each smaller group reports the findings to the entire group.

3. *Case Study.** Detailed information about a problem is presented to a group, or the group members secure the information. The following facts should be included:

a. The people involved.

b. The historical background of the situation.

c. The relationships among persons or groups involved.

d. The religious background and perspective of the situation.

e. The sociological factors involved.

f. The economic factors involved.

g. The educational backgrounds of persons involved.

h. The ethnic origins of the persons involved.

i. The tensions causing the problem.

The group studies all aspects of the problem and proposes a solution. The following questions can be posed:

a. What are the real issues?

b. How has each person contributed to the problem?

c. Why does the problem exist?

d. What biblical, theological, psychological, sociological, and educational principles might assist in suggesting a solution?

Suggest alternative solutions and select the one that seems most satisfactory to the group.

4. *Chain-Reaction Forum.** A problem is posed to the group. The problem is divided into certain issues that relate to it. The group is subdivided into as many groups as there are issues to be considered. Each subgroup discusses in detail its issue of the main problem, and poses questions that they have regarding this issue.

Each subgroup appoints three leaders among its members. One is a quizzer who presents their questions before the entire group to the resource persons who make up a panel. The second leader in each subgroup is called a heckler. His responsibility is to ask further questions of a probing nature after the quizzer has presented his questions. The third leader is a summarizer whose task is to briefly summarize the issues significant to their concerns at the end of the session.

The resource panel members are placed in the front or the center of the room. Each subgroup in turn has the opportunity to pose its questions and further probe the issues with the panel members. After all quizzers and hecklers have had opportunities to participate, the summarizers from each group present their contributions.

5. *Couple Buzzers.** A problem is posed to the group as a whole. Then persons pair off in groups of two. They discuss between themselves possible solutions to the problem. After a designated time, the entire group enters into a discussion of the problem. (Note: Persons thus have an opportunity to test out their ideas with one person prior to sharing with the entire group.)

6. *Play-Reading Talk-Back.** Several members of the group read a play that presents a problem. After the play is read, the

issues presented in it are discussed by the group. Small groups can be formed prior to the discussion by the entire group, if so desired.

7. *Role Playing.** A problem situation is presented to the group. Several members of the group volunteer to take the roles of the persons who are involved in the problem. These persons leave the room for several minutes in order to plan the method of presentation. They act out the problem in a vivid way and during a climactic moment the leader cuts the action. The members of the group then discuss and analyze the role-playing situation and the various roles that were played. Those who played the roles are also given opportunity to react to their feelings about taking the role of another person.

If an adequate solution is not reached, other members of the group can volunteer to take the roles of the persons posed in the problem and continue the same sequence of activities as outlined above.

8. *Simulation Games.* Some problem, such as the gap between generations, is presented in game form. The game simulates the reality of the problem so that persons have an opportunity to empathize with other persons and to become involved with problems without being hurt. The competition involved presents suspense and interest. In all cases, discussion should follow the game. Such questions should be discussed:

a. How did I feel in the role that I played?

b. What objective (s) did the game have?

c. In what way (s) did I change as a result of playing the game?

Simulation games are available on the market. The names of several games are listed in the bibliography at the back of the book.

D. Desired change: TO HAVE FIRSTHAND
EXPERIENCES.

1. *Action Parable.* This provides an experience that is designed to achieve a goal by involving persons in a conflict situation and allowing students to come to their own conclusions about the learning experience. Students learn by doing and by being. (See *Learning through Encounter* by Robert A. Dow, Valley Forge: Judson Press, 1971, for full explanation and more examples of the action parable.)

Two illustrations are presented here to suggest some action parables designed to establish an attitude of trust.

EXERCISE 47

Divide the group into pairs. Ask each pair to hold hands. Request one person to close his eyes tightly and keep them closed for ten minutes. During this time the other person gives him as many kinds of experiences as he can think of without saying a word (for example, feel textures, open doors, feel objects). After the ten minutes, request the persons to change roles for another ten-minute period.

Talk about the experiences of trust and mistrust. Were you able to trust the person? If so, why? If not, why? What does it feel like to be completely dependent upon someone else?

EXERCISE 48

Divide the group into pairs. Ask one person to stand directly behind the other person. Request the one in the front to close his eyes and fall backwards so that the one in back catches him. Now let the persons change places. Talk about the meaning of this experience.

The following action parable is designed to develop an empathy for persons who are excluded from a group.

EXERCISE 49

Have all members of a group sit or stand in a circle except for one who stands outside. Tell the person on the outside to try to get into the circle by using any means he desires except violence.

Talk about the experience. How did it feel to be outside of the group? How did the outsider feel about those who tried to keep him from getting in? How did he feel when he got into the circle? If he did not get in, how did he feel? How did other people feel about him when he got in? What change did this experience make in him as a person? What persons could the members of the group identify with as they were involved in the experience?

Perhaps you or other members of your group could devise your own action parables.

2. *Field Trip.** Members of a group decide on a place which they would like to visit to secure firsthand information. They make preliminary arrangements with persons in charge of the

place to be visited. When visiting the place, they observe carefully and listen intently to what the guide is saying. Questions are asked if desired. After the trip the group analyzes the knowledge that was gained. (Note: Visits can be made to such places as museums, homes, social agencies, municipal organizations, and special locations of a community.)

3. *Mini-Plunge.* Persons visit certain sections of a city in order to observe and "feel" the community life. This visit should take place from 5:00 P.M. to midnight. In teams of two, the persons visit a designated area where they eat, walk the streets, and visit any activity that is in progress. They try to secure a sense of how people live and what their style of life is. In some cases, it will be necessary to have someone familiar with the area go with them.

Some questions for reflection after the experience are as follows:

a. What were the people like? What attitudes were expressed? What purpose do they have in life?

b. Is the church meeting the needs of these people? In what ways?

c. What does it mean to care for these people?

d. What can we do?

4. *Workshop.** Several experts are available for an extended period of time. Each expert deals with one aspect of a main topic. Members of the group meet with the expert who is concerned with the area of their own interest. Brief speeches, demonstrations, discussions, studying, working, and practicing are carried on in each subgroup.

E. Desired change: TO ENCOUNTER BIBLICAL TRUTHS.

1. *Charting.* This experience may be carried on in subgroups or with the entire group. Read the material in one verse or a series of verses in a biblical passage, and ask the group to state the main idea in one sentence or phrase. Continue this procedure until the entire passage is studied. Then try to state in one sentence what the writer was trying to say. If subgroups are used, they may wish to share their insights with the other groups. (Note: This procedure may also be used when studying a book on theology or philosophy.)

2. *Choral Reading.* Divide the Scripture portion that is to be studied into short meaningful phrases, and sometimes into individual words. Ask certain persons to read one phrase and another group to read another phrase. Sometimes a phrase or

word is designated for just one person to read. The passage of Scripture should be typed out so that each person will have a copy. Rather than designate specific names on the copy, indicate Group 1, Group 2, Solo 1, Solo 2, or Men, Women, or any other grouping you desire.

If the Scripture passage has some direct conversations, designate certain persons to read the parts said by the biblical character (s). The entire group can read the introductory parts that do not include direct quotations. (Note: This method of reading the Bible is more interesting and profitable than reading it verse by verse.)

3. *Depth Bible Encounter.** Select a Bible passage that deals with some social issue or a challenge to commitment. Ask each person to write the verse (s) in his own words without using any words used in the passage itself. Groups of four or five persons are formed. In these subgroups, each person in turn shares his paraphrase with the others in the group. There may be need for clarification of meanings. After the sharing is completed, each person should ask himself this question: "If I really took this passage seriously, what would I have to do?" Request that the question be answered in very specific terms such as naming specific persons, specific attitudes, or specific actions. Persons may share their thoughts with others in their small group, if they desire. There may also be some value in sharing some of the significant learnings with the entire group.

4. *Inductive Bible Study.** Study a particular biblical passage by asking the following questions:

a. To whom is the author speaking?

b. In what location is the author speaking?

c. Under what conditions is the author speaking?

d. What is the author saying?

e. Why is the author saying it?

f. How is the author saying it?

Biblical commentaries, dictionaries, concordances, and atlases may be necessary to answer some of the questions. These resources should be used after the students do their own research. Study may be done in the entire group or in small subgroups. Complete the experience by asking what meaning the passage has for us.

5. *Marginal Notes.* Request students to read a Bible passage and make notes in the margin that have the following meanings:

+ I agree.

O I disagree.

— I do not understand.

M It has made a difference in my life.

C It is a challenge to my life.

After individual study, small subgroups can be formed to share their findings. Portions that are difficult to understand may be discussed to help clarify meanings. Resource books may be available for deeper study. If desired, the groups may share with the entire group. (Note: If students are reluctant to make marginal notes, mimeograph the Bible passage for all to use.)

6. *Multiple Readings.* Form groups of five persons. Select a portion of Scripture that is to be studied. Ask one person in each small group to read the passage out loud to the other members of their group. The other members are asked to write down any thoughts that come to their minds as the passage is being read. Suggest that persons be as creative as possible, by writing descriptive words, phrases, or ideas.

Request that a second person in each group read the same Scripture passage aloud to the group and have the other members write down their additional thoughts. (It will be surprising how many new thoughts come to your mind as the passage is read again.) The third, fourth, and fifth persons read the same biblical passage to the others in the group. Thus, each person will hear the passage five times and have four times to write down his thoughts.

Use the phrases and words to discuss the meaning of the passage. A more creative way to proceed is to ask each person to write some creative piece of work that embodies the thoughts that come to his mind when hearing the Scripture. The writing can be in the form of a poem, litany, song, prayer, story, or paraphrase. Share the writings with the entire group. (Note: At least two hours will be needed if creative writing is to be a part of the experience.)

7. *Paraphrasing.* The group, or small subgroups, take a biblical passage and paraphrase the entire passage in a manner which is suitable to the entire group. In the process of paraphrasing, a great deal of give-and-take will be necessary to come to some consensus about the meaning of the passage. At the end of the experience, ask one person to read the entire paraphrase, or ask the group to read it as a choral reading. (Note: Resource books may be used, if desired, to clarify the meaning of the passage.)

8. *Picture Conversations.* Collect pictures of persons from newspapers and magazines and mount them on construction

paper. Select pictures that represent persons of varied backgrounds and different occupations.

Allow each person to select one of the pictures and request that he study it very carefully. Notice the facial expression and try to understand what kind of a person is pictured. Look intensely into the eyes, and notice the expression around the mouth. If his hands are portrayed in the picture, what do they say about him? What do you think he would like? What do you think he would dislike? Try to imagine him as a living person sitting across the table from you.

Select a biblical passage and study it carefully. Then pretend that you are speaking to the person whose picture you have chosen and wish to explain the meaning of the passage to this person with his uniqueness. Write your explanation on a piece of paper.

Now form into pairs. Ask each pair to exchange pictures. Each person is then to take the role of the person whose picture is in his hand. Each one, in turn, reads his message to the other. The other person first listens to the message that is presented to him, then he responds by asking questions or in whatever way he wishes to carry on a conversation.

After the second person follows the same procedure, the pair should talk about how they felt. Also, they may talk about the difference that is necessary in communicating with persons of differing backgrounds. Some of the conversations can be carried on before the entire group, if desired.

F. Desired change: TO EXPRESS ONESELF IN
   CREATIVE WAYS.

Most of the time we feel that we must all be involved in the same kind of activity at the same time during a learning session. This may often be desirable, but sometimes it is also very profitable to give each person an opportunity to express his reaction to a biblical or theological idea through some individual means of self-expression. The following individual approach is helpful.

Select a theme, a topic, or a concept. Talk about its meaning and then give persons an opportunity to express this meaning through one of the following forms of self-expression. (For example, the ideas of alienation, reconciliation, forgiveness, and love could be used.)

1. *Clay Modeling.* The individual molds the clay into a form that expresses an idea. Or, the individual works with the clay, twisting, pulling, and squeezing it until some form emerges.

2. *Collage Creation*. Provide newsprint, paste, scissors, news-papers, magazines, and, if desired, provide scraps of material, buttons, small pieces of wood, yarn, cord, or any small object. Use the newsprint as a base and completely cover the sheet with pictures, words, and/or other objects that illustrate your idea.

3. *Creative Drama*. Prepare spontaneously a drama on the theme that is to be portrayed. Determine the plot and the characters. Select the players and give them the plot and allow the group to act out the story spontaneously before the entire group.

4. *Individual Drawing*. A person draws a picture that portrays an idea. The picture may be a characterization or of a symbolic nature. The pictures may then be shared and their meanings discussed.

5. *Individual Writing*. An idea may be portrayed in some written form. The creation may be a poem, a litany, a written prayer, a story, or some other literary form.

6. *Modern Parables*. A biblical parable is used as a basis. Study the parable carefully to get the full meaning. Think of a situation in our time that simulates the biblical parable. Write the modern parable in contemporary language or in the King James' style.

7. *Music-Art Happening*. The leader provides a variety of art media, such as finger paints, tempera paints, watercolors, clay, crayons, and marking pencils. As music is played in the background, each person is asked to create some art form that expresses one of his feelings. The art forms may center around a theme, if desired. This should be done in silence, except for the background music. At the end of a designated time (at least a half hour) each person is asked to exhibit his creation. If he desires, he may tell the meaning of his art form. This experience may climax in a celebration or service of worship.

8. *Pantomiming*. Portray an idea through bodily movement without using words. Background music may be used, if desired.

9. *Rhythmic Movement*. Take the words of a song which portrays the desired theme and through various rhythmic movements of the body portray the ideas expressed in the song. Use large, sweeping movements since they are more graceful and more meaningful to the onlooker.

10. *Structuring*. Provide for, or ask persons to bring, objects of any kind, such as balls, blocks, stones, or small boxes. Allow the persons to assemble these in some kind of structural form to portray the theme. (Note: Tinker Toys are very useful for this purpose.)

11. *Celebration.* Times of celebration and joy should result from the knowledge of what God has done for us in the past and what he is doing for us now. We can categorize celebrations in two forms:

a. *Historical celebrations* honor the memory of the "happenings of God" throughout the history of the Christian church. For a list of biblical celebrations refer to a Bible dictionary under the headings of "feasts" or "meals," many of which have their counterparts in New Testament times. (For example, Passover and the Lord's Supper; Feast of Weeks and Pentecost, commemorating the coming of the Holy Spirit.) During the study of the postbiblical history of the Christian church, plan for a celebration of significant events, simulating them as closely as possible.

b. *Contemporary celebrations* give expression to what God is doing in our lives today. For example, we can celebrate our own freedom in Christ by "breaking bread together," singing psalms (songs), verbalizing our worship expressions, offering special gifts, and offering ourselves.

The making and displaying of banners is very appropriate at a time of celebration. (Note: Instructions on how to make banners is given under the heading of "Banners" in Chapter 11.)

12. *Worship.* At the close of a session, a worship experience that includes the creative expressions and products of individuals in the group can be very meaningful. For example, if individuals or groups have prepared a litany, prayer, or a poem, these elements can be incorporated in a service of worship. Any art form that has been created can be put on a table in the center of the group or hung on the wall as the center of worship. Pantomime, drama, and rhythmic movement are other ways of incorporating our self-expressions into the worship of God. Offerings of various kinds are appropriate in our worship experiences. Offerings can be given which express in some way our vocations.

A worship service can center around the offering of our lives. Each person is asked to offer one of his possessions, or present some symbolic form or item, at some central place. At times it may be very significant to have persons give some verbal expression of the meaning of their offerings as they present them.

G. Desired change: TO REFLECT ON INNER FEELINGS.

1. *Confrontations.* Sharing inner feelings with another person allows for a depth of understanding of oneself and the other person. Some experiences of confrontation are suggested below.

EXERCISE 50

Close your eyes. Think back as far as you can remember. What was the earliest experience in your life that is vivid to you? Open your eyes and tell this experience to one other person.

EXERCISE 51

Close your eyes. Think back in your life and recall an experience that was extremely formative. In what way did it change your life? How did it help to make you the kind of person that you now are? Open your eyes and tell this experience to one other person.

EXERCISE 52

Close your eyes. Think back in your life and recall an experience when someone really cared about you. How did you know he cared? In what way did it change your life? How did it help to make you the kind of person that you now are? Open your eyes and tell this experience to one other person.

EXERCISE 53

Close your eyes. Think about some religious experience that was meaningful to you. In what way did it change your life? Open your eyes and share this experience with another person.

2. *Space Exploration.* Since our life space is filled with many influences relating to persons and things and aesthetic, ethical, and spiritual experiences, it is sometimes helpful to recall and analyze these experiences. In doing so, close your eyes and recall experiences which have influenced you or are now influencing you. Some persons in the group may wish to share their explorations with others. No person, however, should be forced to share if he does not desire to do so. Usually in an accepting atmosphere, individuals are free to share their life's experiences and their hopes and aspirations. Below are a few exercises that will illustrate some space explorations.

EXERCISE 54

Close your eyes. Imaginatively put yourself inside an enclosed space where you are completely alone, such as inside a large balloon or a large bubble. Contemplate your feelings for a brief time. How do you feel about being alone? Then bring into the inner space someone else for whom you have deep affection. Think how you feel about this person. In your imagination, write these words on the right side of the enclosed space.

Now bring into your inner space someone toward whom you have negative feelings. Ponder how you feel about him. Write these words in imagination on the left side of your inner space. Now open your eyes.

Ask persons to share their pleasant feelings and record them on the chalkboard or newsprint. In like manner, share and record all negative feelings. Talk about these feelings and their meanings to your lives.

EXERCISE 55

Imaginatively allow each person to select an area of space that is completely devoid of any live or inanimate object. Each person selects the form of this area, such as, cubic block, sphere, conical-shaped form, or form with irregular sides of flat and curved surfaces.

Each person closes his eyes. Imaginatively he may change the form of the space area and/or include any person or thing into it to produce a meaningful experience describing some existing situation or some hopeful desires of the future. Open the eyes.

Ask persons to share their area of space with the others and tell what is included in it. No one, however, should be forced to share his space experience with others unless he so desires.

H. Desired change: TO ACCOMPLISH A TASK.

1. *Demonstration — Work Group.** One or more persons demonstrate the operation and use of some kind of equipment or some technique. For example, the operation of a film projector or the use of one of the teaching techniques described in this chapter may be demonstrated. The demonstration involves both audio and visual presentations. Each person is given opportunity to practice the operation of the equipment or to participate in the technique.

2. *Work Group.** The group determines a task that needs to be accomplished. They determine how it is to be accomplished. They determine by whom it is to be accomplished. Subgroups are designated to complete certain aspects of the task, or the entire group works together.

11
What Resources Assist in Change?

There are many, many resources available to an adult teacher and adult groups, and our learning experiences would be more vital and meaningful if we would take advantage of them. The good teacher or leader uses many resources. In this chapter we will discuss the printed page, the audio-visual media, and resource persons. We will conclude the chapter with a discussion of a multimedia approach to learning.

PRINTED RESOURCE MATERIALS

Four kinds of printed resources will be described. They are the Bible, biblical resource books, prescribed curriculum materials, and other books. Each has its own validity and appropriateness according to the needs of the group.

The Bible

Because the Bible is the basis of our Christian faith, it is important that we study the Bible with intense interest and care. Greek and Hebrew scholars study the Bible in the original languages. We should try to learn from their insights. We should also study the Bible in historical perspective and try to derive meaning from it for our lives today.

Biblical Resource Books

To assist us in studying the Bible, there are various resources that can be used.

1. *A Bible concordance* includes a list of words found in the Bible followed by a record of the verses where these words are found. There are some large concordances which list every reference, and some which contain only a brief selection. Some Bibles have brief concordances in the back pages.

2. *A Bible atlas* presents information about the lands where biblical events took place. It usually includes detailed maps and pictures.

3. *A Bible commentary* takes each verse, or series of verses, and gives some explanation of the meaning. There are a few

one-volume commentaries that include the entire Bible, but these, of necessity, have to give very brief interpretation of each passage. Most commentaries consist of many volumes. Since each commentary (or series) tends toward the interpretation of its writer, it is beneficial to have several commentaries on hand to secure several points of view.

4. *A Bible dictionary* contains articles about the main events, words, persons, and locations recorded in the Bible. A brief explanation is given of each item listed, usually followed by or including biblical references to the subject. There is an advantage in having several dictionaries on hand because authors vary in their interpretation of events and some emphasize certain events to the exclusion of others.

5. *A Greek lexicon* is a dictionary that includes and defines words used in the Greek New Testament. Some lexicons begin with the Greek language and define the words in English, whereas others give the English word and then present the Greek word. Some issues of a lexicon include both of these forms.

6. *A Hebrew lexicon* is similar to the Greek lexicon except that it presents words used in the Hebrew Old Testament.

7. *A topical index* presents themes or ideas which are found in the Bible and records the biblical passages where these themes or ideas are found.

Some books contain a combination of the resources listed above. For example, some Bible dictionaries also include a concordance.

Prepared Curriculum Materials

We use the term "curriculum materials" to differentiate the term from the word "curriculum." Curriculum is defined as "the sum of all planned learning experiences under the guidance of the church, directed toward accomplishing the church's mission." [1] Curriculum materials or curriculum resources refer to the printed materials which are prepared for teachers to use as a basis for their teaching program. The curriculum resources contain study materials, goals for the teaching ←→ learning situations, and ways by which the goals might be achieved. Most curriculum materials present additional suggested resources that can be used in the study at hand.

There are two main ways in which curriculum materials approach the study of the Bible. The differentiation between these two ways needs clarification. They are the deductive and inductive approach to Bible study. Since the terms represent diametrically opposed approaches, the differences may be seen in the following chart. However, we can also consider these approaches as points on a continuum so that most curriculum materials represent an approach at some point between these extremes. The differences in approach refer to the method of teaching and the starting point rather than divergent theological viewpoints.

DEDUCTIVE APPROACH	INDUCTIVE APPROACH
1. Begin with general statements and follow with specific examples.	1. Begin with specific examples and follow with general statements that come as a result of examination and study.
2. Begin with a Bible passage and then relate it to life situations.	2. Begin with a problem or an issue and relate biblical truths to it.
3. Facts are presented by the teacher or leader, either to be accepted or discussed by the group.	3. Individuals and/or the group search for information and draw their own conclusions.
4. The student is passive.	4. The student is very much involved in the teaching←→ learning process.
5. The study is content-centered.	5. The study is life or problem-centered.
6. Learning tends to be imposed upon the student by another.	6. Each person does his own learning although he is helped by the group.
7. The teacher/leader uses resources which enrich his own knowledge which he then passes along to the group/class members.	7. The class/group uses the resources before, during, and/ or after the session.
8. The class/group is more dependent upon the teacher/ leader to give guidance.	8. The class/group is more dependent upon its own initiative in guiding members in their decisions.
9. Learning may be unrelated to needs.	9. Learning is done in the context of a life situation which brings meaning to the thing learned.

Obviously, not all curriculum materials fall into such neatly opposed presentations. There is often a combination of the two, but generally writers of curriculum materials tend to slant their approach one way or the other.

Both approaches can be effective if used creatively, but many teachers feel more comfortable with the deductive approach. Neither approach is inherently more biblical than the other. The New Testament Epistles, which give us the main doctrine of the church and our faith, came to us by the inductive method. When churches or individuals were faced with problems, letters were written to them about their particular problems. This process was life-centered learning: it was learning in the context of a situation. How strange, therefore, that many reject the inductive method of teaching because they feel that it is non-biblical in approach!

Other Printed Materials

Printed materials other than the prepared curriculum resources can be used in two different manners. One use is to supplement the study in progress and the other is to use the elective system of study. Let us look at both of these approaches.

Supplemental Resources. When prescribed curriculum materials are used, they should be supplemented with other printed books, magazines, newspapers, or journals. Supplemental resources enrich the curriculum materials and make the teaching ◄─► learning situation more relevant to the needs of the group. The use of these materials means that a teacher/leader is not keeping strictly to a prescribed curriculum but is using some of his own ingenuity to make the teaching ◄─► learning situation more relevant to his class.

Elective Books. When a class or group does not feel that the prescribed curriculum meets its specific needs, the elective principle can be employed. Criteria for selecting elective-type books and resources are listed below.[2]

1. What are the needs of the class/group members?
2. What are the interests of the class/group members?
3. Is adequate time available for the study? If not, could the group meet at another time in order to have a longer period together?
4. What are the learning goals of the class/group which have been agreed upon by the class/group?
   Is the purpose to study a subject or issue in order to take appropriate action?

Is the purpose of the study to gather information only?

How is the study related to the mission of the local congregation?

5. How will the projected study relate to other programs in the total life of the church? Are some important areas of study being overlooked?

Groups may wish to alternate between the use of prepared curriculum materials and of elective books, depending upon the needs of the group.

AUDIO-VISUAL MATERIALS

The ears and the eyes are important organs that assist in the learning process. The use of audio and/or visual means can assist in clarifying words and ideas. Here are twenty-one different kinds of audio-visual materials for your consideration.

1. *Artifacts* are things which are made by human skill or work. They include models and other original creations. Members of the group may possess them or they may be secured from friends or from a museum. Items from various parts of the country or from other countries may enhance a teaching←→learning situation. Artifacts add the additional sense of touch to our learning experience since most of them can be handled in some manner.

2. *Banners* are wall hangings that have inscribed on them some message of significance. Often an art form is also included. Banners may be purchased from religious bookstores or may be made by members of the group. They can be any shape or size, but most banners are oblong and are usually twice as high as they are wide. The simplest and cheapest banner can be made from burlap. Pieces of felt of different colors can be cut out and pasted appropriately on the material so the message can be easily read. The lower edge can be raveled and there can be a small hem on the top edge so that a dowel can be put through it to hang it on the wall.

3. *The chalkboard* can be used to illustrate points and to emphasize ideas. Words that are seen as well as heard fortify the learning. For example, prior to the session, the leader can write the goal for the session on the board so that all will see it on entering the room. The group can react to the goal and change it if so inclined.

4. *Charts* usually show relationships between things. Statistical information can be made more understandable through pictorial form in line, bar, or circular charts. The development of processes or organizations can be pictured in chart form.

5. Action shown in *films* presents a message in a very vivid way. Films should be selected for a purpose and not used merely as a "fill-in."

6. *Filmstrips* present an idea in a series of pictures that have continuity. They are often accompanied by a record that describes or comments on the filmstrip. One value of the filmstrip over the film is that a single frame can be kept on the screen and discussed if it has special significance.

7. *Maps* are very valuable in showing geographical locations of events that are being discussed.

8. *Mobiles* contain pieces of metal, wood, or cardboard that are suspended on wires or threads so that they are evenly balanced and move in a slight breeze. The hanging objects may be letters, words, designs, pictures mounted on cardboard, or symbols that describe some theme.

9. *Music* with or without words, can be listened to, or it can be used as background for some other learning aid. Music can have a great effect upon persons. It can soothe, it can irritate, it can energize, it can challenge. Select the type of music according to the purpose you wish to achieve.

At times, persons will want to sing along with the accompaniment, bringing greater participation to the experience.

10. *Newsprint* can be used in the same manner as a chalkboard. The newsprint has the additional advantage that sheets can be torn off as they are filled and put elsewhere on the wall with masking tape for later referral, and if desired, can be kept for use in other sessions.

11. *Photographs* taken by professionals and amateurs can be used to good advantage. If they are small, they may be shown in an opaque projector so that all will be able to see.

12. *Pictures* may be cut from magazines or newspapers, and mounted on construction paper. Professional prints of pictures are also valuable. Some of the great paintings are available for purchase at art museums for small sums. Libraries or museums rent pictures or sometimes loan them with no fee attached.

13. *Projections in an opaque projector* may be used to present books, magazines, pictures, charts, letters, and typewritten materials. These resources can be projected on a screen.

14. *Radio programs* can be the basis of discussion. The teacher/leader should be aware of significant programs that stimulate ideas and thought.

15. *Records* of music or speaking can stimulate discussion. Members of the group may have records that they wish to share.

16. *Slides* that are purchased or taken by members of the group may be illustrative of the topic being studied.

17. *Symbols* used by the Christian church, such as the vine or the cross, can be very significant teaching aids. Each symbol is full of meaning. Often a knowledge of the historical significance of the symbol will add to its value. Symbols are often found in pictures or are included in stained-glass windows and other parts of the church sanctuary.

18. *Tape recordings* of speeches, panel discussions, or other similar events can be helpful in the study of a particular problem. Complete tapes need not be played. Using just a portion of the tape may be much more effective than a prolonged speech.

Tape recordings of music can also be used either to study the music or as background music during the session.

19. *A television program* held at the time of the regular class session can be shared with the entire group. When a significant television program is to be shown at a time different from the class session, some members may wish to gather in homes or at the church, view the program together, and then share their reactions with one another.

20. *Transparencies for an overhead projector* can be prepared in advance or may be made during the session. The overhead projector can be used in a well-lighted room and is placed in the front of the room. The image is projected behind the projector.

21. *Video tape* records sound and picture simultaneously and can be played back immediately. Special events in the life of the church or of the community can be recorded and shown to the group for study. The video tape can be used in the classroom as well. The class session can be recorded and played back later to study its effectiveness.

Many of the audio-visual materials listed above can be made by the class members. This involvement of the members will create more interest and therefore more learning.

MULTIMEDIA LEARNING

The more senses that are involved in a learning experience the greater possibility there is that real learning will take place. The multimedia approach brings several senses into play when dealing with an issue or a problem. Such an approach can be used in two different ways: one approach is to have a sequence of activities which use a different medium for each activity;

the other approach uses several media simultaneously. We will discuss both of these uses.

Sequence of Media

Some English teachers in the public school devised a multi-media approach to learning and Carolyn Goddard has adapted it for use in Christian education.[3]

Six distinct media are suggested which include the following experiences:

1. *Body* — includes all sensory experiences, pantomime, creative drama.
2. *Sight* — includes art, graphics, drawings, sculpture, slides, photographs, pictures, and the like.
3. *Sound* — Includes speech, noise, music.
4. *Sight-Sound* — Includes films, filmstrips, television, videotape.
5. *Print* — Includes reading and writing.
6. *Experience* — Includes action as a result of the learning.

In addition, each of the six media has a reactive and an active phase.

The *reactive phase* involves things that the teacher does and the students react to:

the students
- hear or listen,
- look at something shown to them,
- read,
- think.

The *active phase* involves things that the student himself produces:

the students
- speak,
- write,
- produce some object.

Combining or involving all of these experiences in a total learning situation involves the learner as a whole person and gives him an opportunity to express his learning through some action. Such a sequence of activities would, of necessity, take place over a series of sessions, but the totality of the experience produces involvement, interest, and total response throughout all of the sessions.

To illustrate the totality of the experience, educators have suggested the form of the wheel and have diagrammed it as shown below.

When a teacher creates a wheel, he is really creating two wheels:

1. *The presentation-wheel* which involves the reactive phase wherein the student is confronted with audio and visual materials to which he reacts; and

2. *The problem-wheel* which generates problems which the student can solve using the various media. This involves the active phase.

Let us illustrate this concept by taking the theme of love and showing some experiences that could be planned to express this theme.

REACTIVE	ACTIVE
1. *Body.* All persons stand in a circle with shoulders touching. Request each individual to express love toward the persons on either side of them in a nonverbal manner.	1. *Body.* Express feelings of love through pantomime or creative drama.
2. *Sight.* Show a picture of Christ's crucifixion illustrating his great love for us.	2. *Sight.* Make a collage that shows persons showing love to others.
3. *Sound.* Play a record of an appropriate song, such as "O Love That Will Not Let Me Go."	3. *Sound.* Sing the song that was played, or create other words to the song and sing it.
4. *Sight-Sound.* Show a film or show the filmstrip "In Faith and Love."	4. *Sight-Sound.* Illustrate the song sung above with slides or pictures made or arranged by the group.
5. *Print.* Read a Bible passage about love, perhaps 1 Corinthians 13.	5. *Print.* Paraphrase the words of the chapter read from the Bible.
6. *Experience.* Visit a children's hospital or a convalescent home to see how others show love to those in need.	6. *Experience.* In some concrete act, show love to some person or group of persons.

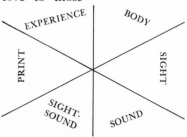

In contrast to the sequential pattern of various media illustrated above, there is also an effective presentation of material when more than one medium is used simultaneously. The group should select a single theme and determine which media they will be using. Several illustrations are given here.

1. A film can be shown in the center of the room. At one side of the film, slides can be shown in rapid succession. At the other side of the film, a filmstrip can be shown. If the sound of the film would be distracting, do not use it and substitute some appropriate background music. Intersperse with brief statements or Scripture passages, if desired.

2. Excerpts from three films can be shown simultaneously and the sound can be alternated.

3. Shadow pictures which are projected on a screen can be shown simultaneously with slides and appropriate music.

The combinations of media are limitless. Experiment with different backgrounds on which to project the films, slides, or filmstrips. Use such things as curtains, the wall, venetian blinds, the ceiling, or burlap. Various kinds of lighting, such as strobe lights, or a color wheel can also give special effects.

This kind of multimedia presentation totally involves a person in an experience. The impact of the message is powerful.

RESOURCE PERSONS

A special speaker can be asked to come to the class and present material on a particular subject in which he is especially knowledgeable. Panel members and symposium speakers can add to a learning situation. Guests can be asked to participate in an interview. Persons of different professions or different religions can provide helpful information.

Some guests can be requested to visit a class or group as resource persons and not speakers. In this capacity, the guest participates in the discussion as do all other members of the group. He may, however, be asked to give special insight into some problem because of his special knowledge of the subject.

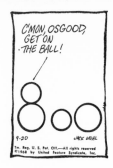

12
How Do We Plan for Change?

Change does not come automatically; we must plan for it. We will consider first the needs of a person who is planning a structured learning situation, and then discuss the needs of a person who is challenged by an unstructured learning experience. The structured learning situation involves a teacher who uses prescribed curriculum materials as a basis for a study, while the unstructured learning situation involves a teacher/leader who develops, with his students/group members, learning experiences which are dependent upon the immediate needs of the group and are planned as the study or experience develops. We shall conclude the chapter with a look at team teaching.

PLANNING FOR STRUCTURED LEARNING EXPERIENCES

A person who is using prescribed curriculum materials which include a study book or quarterly for both teacher and student already has a good start in the planning process. In fact, someone else has already done some of his planning for him. What has been done, however, is only preliminary planning, and every teacher needs to plan for his own class.

Curriculum materials
    are tools for the teacher to use;
        they are not chains to which teachers are bound.

Each person in a group is an individual, and each group of persons is unique. Each teacher should do his own planning so that the needs of his group are met.

When a teacher secures the curriculum materials which he is to use, he should read the entire teacher's and student's books before he does any planning. He then considers whether he will follow the suggested plan of study or will adjust the study to meet certain purposes that are more relevant to his group. For instance, he may decide that some sessions may need more time than prescribed and perhaps some sessions could be eliminated. He may also decide that he does not want to use all the materials.

There is definite value in preparing a unit plan, which briefly outlines the goals and learning experiences for the entire series of sessions. This plan will assist you in evaluating the total experience, will give you an opportunity to include variety in the sessions, and will assist in planning for special resource persons and audio-visual or other resource materials.

When you begin planning for the immediate session at hand, there are eleven questions to be asked.

1. *What interests and/or needs do the members of your class have?* You will need to know your students well. You may wish to ask them to indicate their particular needs and/or interests in relation to the study to be discussed.

When students are given their study books, they can be asked to glance at the table of contents and to skim through the book. Then ask them what topics are of interest to them. They may even suggest topics that they would like to have eliminated and may recommend alternate topics.

2. *What kinds of changes are desired?* The desired changes should be specifically stated. First, however, you must consider what kinds of changes you should be seeking. Should they involve knowing, feeling, or doing? Or all three? (Refer to the section entitled "What Kinds of Changes?" in chapter 3 and to the entire fourth chapter entitled: "What Changes Are Desired?") There is value in having the class members assist in developing goals.

3. *What kinds of learning experiences are appropriate in bringing about the desired changes?* Here you need to consider the student and how he will become involved. It is desirable to request students to give their suggestions.

4. *What resources are available for your use?* Here you can consider a wide variety of resources such as books, audiovisuals, and resource persons. (Refer to chapter 11.) Many teachers' books include a list of resources at the end of each session or at the back of the book.

5. *What techniques can assist in bringing about the desired changes?* Remember our rule: We use lecture only as a last resort. (Refer to chapters 9 and 10.)

6. *How will you motivate for learning?* If you have involved the students in the planning thus far, they will already be motivated. You may wish to stimulate their thinking by asking questions to be considered at the next session or by giving specific assignments for individual research. In planning for the actual session, it is important to begin it with some kind of activity that will arouse the interest of the participants.

7. *How will you plan for crossing points to take place?* How will the gospel intersect the needs of individuals? How will the Bible be used? How can a student be given opportunities to apply the Christian faith to life situations so that changes will take place in his knowledge, attitudes, and actions? (Refer to chapter 7.)

8. *What will be the sequence of the learning activities or experiences?* How will you begin the session? How will you develop the topic to involve the students? How will you conclude the session? How will you motivate the students for the next session?

9. *How much time should be allotted to each activity?* The preceding question dealt with a sequence of activities, but it is also necessary to estimate a time for each learning activity. This estimate will enable you to evaluate whether you have too much or too little planned for the time allotted for your session.

One problem that teachers often have when they use prescribed materials is due to their feeling that they should use all the suggestions presented. Remember that the printed materials are merely suggestive, and you have the responsibility to select those activities which will suit the needs of your group and fit into the time that is allotted to you. Some suggestions in the material may not be appropriate for your situation, in which case you will not use them.

You may wish to plan for extended times for study if the time allotted to you is not adequate. You may even wish to meet at another time if that is suitable to the class members.

If you are planning student involvement, at least one hour is needed for learning, but this period is too long if only lecture is used.

10. *What room arrangement is needed to provide a good climate for learning?* The arrangement of the room is very important to the success of the teaching←→learning situation. Chairs may be arranged in a circle, around tables, or in a semicircle depending upon the activity. The teacher needs to come early to set up the room so that he can speak to students as they come into the class.

11. *How will you determine what kind of changes have taken place?* Before the class session begins it will be necessary to determine how you will evaluate what has taken place during the session. Some kind of evaluative process should take place at the end of each class or group session. These activities may be of a formal or informal nature. (Refer to chapter 13.)

Several of the following principles can be applied to the questions listed above.

1. *Use variety in planning your sessions.* Some persons feel comfortable in having the same sequence of activities each session. Usually these people resist change of any kind. On the other hand, there are others who dislike a routine and demand variety in order to keep their interest. Variety in learning experiences will assist in keeping a class alive in more ways than one. It will keep a class from "dying" by keeping persons interested enough to come to the class. Variety will also give "life" to the class in terms of enthusiasm and interest. More learning will probably take place when variety is used than when a class is carried on with a routine procedure.

2. *Involve the students in the teaching◄─►learning process.* Students learn or change only when they are involved. One of the most important questions to answer is: "How can I involve my students?"

3. *Not everyone needs to be involved in the same way.* Sometimes several learning possibilities should be offered in one session. Then the students may select the learning experience in which they would like to be involved. Small groups and individuals can be working simultaneously on their activities and share their learnings with the entire group at the end of the session. This procedure allows for individual differences and will result in enriching experiences for all involved.

4. *Consider the whole person when planning.* Since individuals are not compartmentalized into segments of being but are whole persons, it is important to plan so that all aspects of their being will be affected.

5. *Be flexible in carrying out your plans.* Although careful planning is necessary, to follow a plan slavishly defies good teaching principles. Be sensitive to the group and adjust plans as situations demand.

PLANNING FOR UNSTRUCTURED LEARNING EXPERIENCES

In an unstructured learning experience there are no prescribed curriculum materials, and the leader and group develop their own plan, select their own resources, and determine their own plan of procedure. There are several ways that the unstructured learning experience differs from the structured one. Four characteristics of the unstructured experience are listed below.

1. *The group as a whole is involved in the planning process.*

The teacher/leader guides the planning process but works with others in the group. One of the main purposes of an unstructured learning experience is to involve persons where they are and, in order to do this, there must be involvement of all in the planning process. The same eleven questions that were asked in planning a structured learning experience are applicable to group planning but should be answered by the group rather than by one or two persons.

2. *The leadership of the group is shared by all.* There is usually a designated leader, but all members of the group are responsible for carrying out activities that assist in achieving the goals or desired changes. We use the term "leadership" as anything that is done to assist in achieving the goals set by the group. Everyone is responsible to do this, not just the designated leader.

In some groups the role of designated leader rotates from person to person as the group decides. The designated leader assumes the role of a moderator who assists others in their participation.

3. *The goals are constantly under evaluation.* Although the learning experiences are unstructured in some respects, a group needs to have goals to guide them. These goals are determined by the group members. The goals, however, are constantly kept before the group, and as the group matures, they may feel the necessity of changing their goals to fit their immediate needs. This flexibility keeps the group vital, alive, and relevant.

4. *The group must be small in order to be effective.* A small learning group consists of from eight to fifteen persons. The unstructured situation can only be dealt with in the small group because the complete involvement of all and the necessity of interaction between persons demand a small group.

Although we have made a strict demarcation between the structured and unstructured learning experiences, this distinction does not always need to be so. There are times when elements of both kinds of experience are appropriate.

Some groups are not ready for unstructured learning experiences; their past experiences demand some structure. Sometimes it is necessary to begin with a structured experience and when confidence and trust develop, the group will be ready to try a more unstructured experience. This maturity will partly depend upon the leader of the structured group. He must be ready to risk working in an unstructured learning experience before he can challenge the others in the group to risk.

We will describe three different kinds of unstructured learning groups: the discussion group, the personal growth group, and the action group.

1. *The discussion group* using the unstructured form decides on its own topics for discussion. At the end of each meeting time the group decides on the topic to be discussed at its next meeting. It will also decide on the designated leader for that discussion topic.

The informal discussion group might be composed of people who have common needs but are interested in exploring these needs in an unstructured manner. Groupings may take the form of interracial dialogues, ecumenical dialogues, community issue conversations, adult-youth dialogues, and so forth.

The designated leader will prepare tentative goals and a tentative outline for discussion, allow the group to adjust these at the beginning of the session, and guide the group in achieving the goals.[1] He will also have responsibility for determining an evaluation procedure at the end of the session.

2. *The personal growth group* is designated by other names, such as personal encounter group, listening group, and learning group.[2] Such groups all involve the concept of experiential education where persons become involved in some learning experience from which they draw their own conclusions. Thus, the learning is experienced by the person and is not imposed upon him.

Personal growth is achieved through a person-oriented experience of interrelationships among persons. In order for change to take place, there must be acceptance of persons, an expression of an *agape* type of love, an openness to each other, and a sensitivity to God's purposes. (Refer to chapter 8 for principles of working in groups.)

Most personal growth groups have a "trainer" who provides the kinds of learning experiences that open persons to themselves, to others, and to God. Some personal growth groups are called T-Groups (training groups) that are usually completely unstructured.[3] Such groups need trained leadership. Encounter tapes are available for the self-directed group, but there are certain specifications designated for groups using these tapes.[4]

3. *Action groups* meet for the purpose of carrying out the biblical injunction:

"Do not fool yourselves by just listening to [God's] word. Instead, put it into practice" (James 1:22, TEV).

A commitment to act, in addition to a commitment to know

and to feel, should be encouraged wherever it may be appropriate.

Four elements are involved in developing a plan of action.[5] They are as follows:

1. *Assumptions* are the underlying premises upon which objectives and strategy are based. Three different kinds of assumptions need to be considered:

   a) *Environmental:* those about the world in which we live.

   b) *Theological:* statements about God, man, salvation, mission, church, ministry, and so forth.

   c) *Operational:* policy statements which indicate the way the group wishes to act.

2. *Objectives* are the goal(s) toward which the action is to be directed.

3. *Strategy* is a general course of action which is selected to achieve the goal(s).

4. *Tactics* are the specific steps to be undertaken to implement the strategy.

When action is taken, a period of reflection is needed to consider questions like these:

— Were our assumptions valid?

— Were our objectives realistic? Were they achieved? Do we need to restate our objectives?

— Was our general strategy effective? Whom did we reach? How was it done?

— What is our next step?

Since action is our goal, there is a danger of becoming too task-oriented and forgetting about persons in the process. No task is so important that persons should be disregarded. Relationships within the group, which are the primary concern of the personal growth group, are also important in action groups, although they are not primary.

TEAM TEACHING

It has been said:

Two heads are better than one.

That statement is applicable to teaching. A person who assumes complete responsibility for the teaching⟷learning process cuts himself off from the enriching experience of working together with another person as a team. Two or three persons who work together provide additional insight for each other about persons, objectives, methods of procedure, and evaluation. Vitality, creativity, and support of persons are some results of team teaching.

Team teaching needs to be differentiated from the use of an assistant teacher. The team works together in three phases of the teaching process.

1. *The team plans together.* All planning is done by the members of the team. During the planning process the persons determine who is to assume certain responsibilities prior to and during the class session. The team members will work separately to fulfill these tasks.

2. *The team teaches together.* All members of the team should be actively involved in each session. There are many ways that this can be carried out. Several ways are:
— One person can assume primary responsibility for leadership and another can assist.
— Primary leadership can be rotated every other session.
— Primary leadership can be rotated every other month or every other quarter, or on some other regular basis.
— One member of the team can assume responsibility for the leadership of the class and another member can be an observer, watching closely how persons interact with each other, who responds, how they respond, and similar matters.

3. *The team evaluates together.* After each session the members of the team need to evaluate what has taken place before planning for the next session. Whenever possible and feasible, some specific evaluation procedures should be used that give reactions from members of the group rather than just impressions by the team members. (Refer to chapter 13.)

I'LL SAY THIS MUCH FOR NORMAN... HE'S GOT A DIFFERENT SLANT ON THINGS.

13
Has Change Taken Place?

Meet Miss T and Mr. U

Miss T and Mr. U are team teachers. Each week they plan together. One of their important tasks is to evaluate what has been happening in their class. They usually follow the procedure that when one is the main leader for the day, the other person pays particular attention to the kinds of interactions that are taking place. This information is then shared after the session. Several times they have used a Postmeeting Reaction Form where the class members were asked to write their reactions about the class session. This procedure worked out quite well, and they found that they were learning quite a bit about their teaching effectiveness. They feel they would like to do more of this kind of evaluation, but they don't want to do the same thing all of the time. They are eager to learn new ways of evaluating.

In evaluation we review the task in relation to the goals that we have set for ourselves. Evaluation helps us see if the goals have been achieved. We can ask ourselves the questions:

Have the desired changes taken place?

To what degree have these changes taken place?

(Miss T and Mr. U always carefully plan the goals for each session, but they never thought of evaluation in the light of these goals. Now that they are aware of this need, they can make their evaluations more purposeful.)

SOME WAYS OF EVALUATING

Evaluation can be done in a variety of ways. Equipment is needed for some of the ways and sometimes mimeographed forms are used. Let us look at various ways to see how they can be used.

1. *A designated observer.*

When members of a group are consciously trying to improve their skills in discussion, they may wish to designate one or two persons in the group as observers. The observer sits back from the group and does not participate verbally in the discussion, but instead observes what is going on in the group. When this procedure is followed, time should be allowed at the end of the session for the observer(s) to report. Time should also be allotted for the reactions from the group to the observer's report.

There are a variety of things that an observer can do. Let us consider these in detail.

(Miss T and Mr. U have done some observing themselves, but as yet they have not been brave enough to ask someone in the group to observe. They are not sure, either, that the class is ready for this step, but they have decided to try soon.)

a. *Questions for consideration:* A list of questions can be prepared in advance so that the observer will know what to observe. Here are a few suggestions:

(1) Is the atmosphere tense or relaxed?
(2) Is the goal clear?
(3) Are the participants helping to achieve the goal? In what ways?
(4) How is the leader affecting the group?
(5) How is the group affecting the leader?
(6) Are persons assisting others to contribute? How?
(7) Are persons listening to each other?
(8) Is there eye contact?
(9) What situations hinder the discussion?
(10) What situations help the discussion?

b. *Numerical recording.* The observer can record the number of times that each person spoke during the discussion. A list of the persons in the group is made and each time a person speaks a mark is recorded behind his name. Any kind of verbal utterance should be thus recorded. At the end of the discussion time, the marks can be tabulated and reported. In some groups the names may not be used, but only the number of people who spoke a certain number of times will be reported; for example, an observer could say: "Three speople spoke twenty-eight times, two people spoke ten times." This report presents actual data and not merely assumptions.

c. *Flow chart.* Flow charts can be made in several ways. Such a chart should always show the seating arrangement of the members of the group. The flow of conversation can be charted by drawing a line from the first person who speaks to the next person who speaks and continuing this procedure throughout the entire discussion time. The completed chart will give a pictorial demonstration of how the conversation flowed and where the concentrations were in the discussion. It will also show the degree to which the group is dependent upon the leader for carrying the discussion.

Charts can also be made to indicate which persons talked

to whom and whether or not the other person responded. This chart may be made by drawing arrows between the persons who are speaking and the persons to whom they are speaking. The person who initiated the conversation between two persons can be designated by a small line that crosses near the arrowhead by his name. When remarks are directed to the group as a whole, the arrow is pointed into the middle of the circle rather than to a particular person.

When the group observes these charts, they can analyze the flow of conversation and what this flow means to the success of the group.

d. *Timing*. A person can record the length of time that persons speak. Group discussions are not times for lengthy speeches; so the actual recording of the length of individual contributions will provide some data for discussion.

The time needed for persons to become involved can also be recorded. Often the beginning of a discussion shows some lag in dealing with issues. A person with a watch can record the length of time that it took the group to reach certain crucial stages in the progress of the discussion or how long it took to reach a group decision.

e. *Listing phrases*. A person can record verbatim some specific statements made that have significance to the progress or the hindrance of the discussion. These phrases can be reported to the group at the end of the discussion and comments can be made about the effect the statements had on the group or on an individual in the group.

f. *Listing first part of sentences*. A person can record the first few words in each sentence that is made by each contributor. These phrases can be listed in sequence and perhaps put on a piece of newsprint. The first part of a sentence can have a great deal of significance to the response others have to what he is saying. For example, a contribution beginning with the words: "I *still* say that . . ." could bring negative reactions, for to some the statement could mean that this person is not listening to what is being said and/or is not willing to change. Of course, the tonal qualities that are used play a great part in reactions from the group.

There are some cautions that should be noted as the observer reports the results to the members of the group.

(1) *Present the information in a nonpersonal manner.* Avoid using names, especially in a group that is not cohesive and where some persons might be extremely sensitive.

(2) *Present only that information which is needed.* Too much information presented to a group may confuse them rather than assist them in understanding how the information affected the group's progress.

(3) *Present only that information which the group is ready to receive.* Be sensitive to persons who might be easily offended. Also be sensitive to the kind of issues that can be dealt with by the group.

(4) *Present a good balance of praise and confrontation.* It is good to report instances where good teamwork was in evidence, but groups also need to know areas that showed lack of good teamwork. A good balance between the two will make for a good response.

(5) *Present observations in a nonjudgmental manner.* Report only the facts and leave the interpretations to the members of the group. If one judges or preaches to the group, some will become defensive and consequently the information will not be helpful to them.

(6) *Describe situations rather than attack persons.* The role which a person has played should be described without making judgmental statements about his behavior.

Usually observations are reported at the end of the discussion. There are times, however, when the group might ask for an observer's report during the discussion. This request is appropriate especially when the group is lagging in interest or is not working toward its goal.

2. *Tape recorder.*

A tape recorder can be placed in the room so that the discussion can be taped and recorded for future playback. This procedure gives specific data which can be helpful. Personal observations are not always completely accurate; so the tape can give more specific evidence of what has happened. Such things as tonal qualities, inflections of the voice, when people laughed, and things people say can be checked by listening to the tape at a later date.

The teacher/leader may use the tape for his own purpose, but it should also be used to play back to individuals, small groups, or the entire group as the need demands.

(Mr. U has a tape recorder that he uses for many purposes, but he never thought of using it to tape the class sessions. He wonders how the class members will react to speaking into a microphone, but he and Miss T are going to try it soon.)

125

3. Video tape.

The additional value the video tape has over the tape recording is that it not only records the words that people say but also visually records the scene. The television playback can be useful in seeing facial expressions and bodily movements, as well as listening to what people have said.

(No video tape machine is available at the church where Miss T and Mr. U teach. They have heard, however, that sometimes one is available at Adult Laboratory Schools. This technique is something they can keep in mind for the future. Maybe their church will decide to purchase a machine for other purposes and they could use it occasionally.)

4. Interviews.

Special persons can be interviewed personally after the session to secure reactions from them. Care should be taken not to ask only those persons who might give favorable comments. Their comments are needed, but feedback also is needed from the more critical persons, those who might have "a chip on their shoulders."

(Miss T has decided to take the list of class members and designate dates for each member to be interviewed. She has decided at times to inform certain of the persons before the session that she or Mr. U will be interviewing them after the class.)

5. Ranking.

If a group has become harmoniously united by common interests and members are secure enough to try ranking each other in terms of some standard, they can secure some very valuable information about themselves by asking the following questions:

a. If you were going to give a party, who in the group would be first on your list of persons whom you would invite? Rate others in ranking order.

b. If you were stranded on the highway, whom would you wish to stop and help you? Rank others in order of your preference.

c. Who was most helpful in our discussion today? Rate persons in ranking order.

Each person can be asked the question and his answers can be written on a piece of paper. However, one person can be selected from the group and he can request the persons to line up in the center of the room as he calls their names. The leader can then ask the persons at various points in the line how they feel about where they were placed. The person who ranked them can also present his reason for placing the persons as he ranked them.

(Miss T and Mr. U feel that their class would not be ready for this kind of an evaluation procedure. They feel that the group members should know each other better than they do. Perhaps at a later time at a social gathering of the class it might be a good time to try it.)

6. Reflections.

Persons in the group can be asked to reflect on some incident(s) in their lives that are significant. They may be requested to share these reflections with the group or may be given time to reflect silently upon their own thoughts. These reflections may be for their own growth and a time for meditation between themselves and God.

Occasionally there is a great deal of value in having times of reflection when we have the opportunity to think and reflect on past experiences or possible alternative actions or ways of thinking. Throughout this book there are suggested experiences of reflection which might be used.

Since acceptance is such an important part of learning, we offer an experience of reflection that allows one to reflect on his own reactions to certain phrases.

ACCEPTANCE SCALE

Do you feel that you are being accepted as a person of worth when the following phrases are directed to you? (Mark Y for yes and N for no.)

_____ 1. You cannot do that.

_____ 2. Calm down.

_____ 3. You ought not to say such things.

_____ 4. You'd better not try that.

_____ 5. With your permission I would like to rephrase what you have said.

_____ 6. I wish you would do this.

_____ 7. I am counting on you to speak clearly.

_____ 8. I regret that we do not have time to hear what you have to say.

_____ 9. Perhaps you would like to talk about something else.

_____10. That was a stupid thing to say.

_____11. You are not being cooperative.

_____12. That was a good idea.

_____13. If I understand you correctly, the main point you want to drive home is this.

_____14. I always thought you knew better.

_____15. I still say that I am right.

Refl ect on the statements above. What kinds of statements do you contribute in a group? Are they the kinds that show acceptance of persons? Reword the statements that you have marked with an "N" so that they would incite a feeling of acceptance.

7. *Postmeeting reaction forms.*

Forms can be prepared in advance, usually in mimeograph form, to secure information about the reaction of group members to the session just completed. If you wish to make your own forms, here are some of the ways you can ask questions.

a. *Multiple choice.* An example of a multiple-choice question is: How do you feel about today's session? Check the appropriate answer:

_____ Very comfortable

_____ Quite comfortable

_____ So-so

_____ Rather uneasy

_____ Terrible

b. *Direct questions.* Here are two examples of questions that might be asked:

What did you like about today's session?

What insights did you gain from this session?

c. *Listing.* An example of listing is as follows:

List at least three ways in which you think the class can be improved.

d. *Open-end questions.* An open-end question may be stated in the following ways:

The leader made me feel like I was _____.

Today I think that _____ helped me most in clarifying my thoughts.

e. *Checklist.* Here is one way that a checklist question may be stated:

How do you feel that the class might be improved? Select as many items as you think appropriate.

_____ More discussion.

_____ More lecture.

_____ More clarification of items.

_____ More people become involved.

_____ Less domination by some persons.

_____ Select another topic for study.

f. *Rating scale.* Rating a series of choices is illustrated as follows:

What topics would interest you? Rate in order of preference, numbering your first choice "1," your second choice "2," and so on.

_____ Study a book of the Bible.

_____ Study Bible history.

_____ Study church history.

_____ Study the Christian home.

_____ Study the racial crisis.

_____ Study a political issue.

_____ Study the needs of our community.

g. *Charts.* Refer to Postmeeting Reaction Forms B, E, and J in Appendix B.

h. *Time sequence.* A series of questions may be asked at different times during the session.

For example, at the beginning of the session you might want to ask: What are your expectations of the class session today? At the end of the session you might want to ask: In what ways were your expectations fulfilled? Questions also may be asked at other times during the session. Refer to Postmeeting Reaction Form B in Appendix B, where group members are asked to respond to their feelings five different times during the session.

In the specific Postmeeting Reaction Forms given in Appendix B, other illustrations of each of the items listed above will be presented.

(Miss T and Mr. U have used some simple Postmeeting Reaction Forms and are excited about the possibility of trying some new ones. They were not aware of the many different kinds that could be used.)

USING EVALUATION FOR CHANGE

Various types of evaluation are of little value unless we use the information which we received for our future growth. These guidelines are:

— Examine the information as objectively as possible.

— Determine what information is valid for you.

— Examine causes of past behavior.

— Determine what new behaviors should be tried.

In making decisions to change, remember the importance of faith:

— You must have faith in yourself.

— You must have faith in others.

— You must have faith in God.

This kind of faith will bring new life to you.

YOU CAN BE A DIFFERENT PERSON

"Offer yourselves as a living sacrifice to God, dedicated to his service and pleasing to him. This is the true worship that you should offer" (Romans 12:1, TEV).

"Do not conform outwardly to the standards of this world, but let God transform you inwardly by a complete change of your mind. Then you will be able to know the will of God—what is good, and is pleasing to him, and is perfect" (Romans 12:2, TEV).

"Dear friends! Let us love one another, for love comes from God. Whoever loves is a child of God and knows God. Whoever does not love does not know God, because God is love. This is how God showed his love for us; he sent his only Son into the world that we might have life through him" (1 John 4:7-9, TEV).

". . . There is nothing in all creation that will ever be able to separate us from the love of God which is ours through Christ Jesus our Lord" (Romans 8:39, TEV).

"When anyone is joined to Christ he is a new being: the old is gone, the new has come. All this is done by God, who through Christ changed us from enemies into his friends, and gave us the task of making others his friends also" (2 Corinthians 5:17-18, TEV).

Evaluation is an important part of teaching. It must be a constant process and not something that is done at the end of a unit of study. It is a process by which we determine whether or not our goals have been achieved. Have the desired changes taken place?

The teacher needs to analyze himself as well as what is happening to his students. Active participation of students in the evaluative process gives feedback to the teacher. The designated observer in the class provides students with experience and insight in observing the forces at work in the group. Postmeeting Reaction Forms are helpful in securing student reaction for the future growth and planning of the teacher.

AN OPEN LETTER TO AN ADULT TEACHER

My dear artist: (Yes, that means you)

You may not have thought of your work as a teacher as that of an artist, but doesn't it excite you to be considered that way? While the artist works on canvas and the sculptor works with clay, you are working with persons.

As the artist works on canvas, as a teacher you put on strokes of color, you draw lines of meaning, you shade in spots that need to be recessed, you highlight areas that need to be brought to the forefront, all for the purpose of "drawing out" a masterpiece: a person dedicated to Jesus Christ.

As the sculptor works on a piece of clay that has texture and its own peculiarities, the persons with whom you work are individuals with specific characteristics and needs. The person, however, in the hands of the artist is willing to yield to the artist's touch, as he is smoothed in one place, gouged in another, and gently molded to help create a thing of beauty and worth.

God bless you in your task.

Sincerely,
A fellow artist

Appendix A

SELF-RATING SCALE FOR TEACHERS/LEADERS

Read carefully each statement, and then think frankly and objectively about the extent to which you possess the quality or carry out the activity described. Put a circle around the appropriate number that follows the statement, 0 being the lowest rating and 5 the highest. Note the points at which you are weakest and direct your main efforts toward strengthening these.

1. I try to discover the problems, needs, and interests of each person in the group.   0 1 2 3 4 5

2. I try to help everyone feel secure and confident in the group.   0 1 2 3 4 5

3. I try sufficiently to help each individual feel that he is needed by the group as a whole and that he may share or bring up problems as he wishes.   0 1 2 3 4 5

4. I have a real sense of relationship with God and his purpose.   0 1 2 3 4 5

5. I allow others to differ with me without being defensive.   0 1 2 3 4 5

6. I tolerate differences of opinions and even welcome them.   0 1 2 3 4 5

7. I allow members of the group to develop their own goals.   0 1 2 3 4 5

8. I do not attack persons as individuals.   0 1 2 3 4 5

9. I have clearly defined goals.   0 1 2 3 4 5

10. I have faith in myself, without being arrogant.   0 1 2 3 4 5

11. I have faith in members of the group.   0 1 2 3 4 5

12. I never assume anything.   0 1 2 3 4 5

13. I am patient with members of the group.   0 1 2 3 4 5

14. I accept the feelings of others as valid.   0 1 2 3 4 5

15. I know when to keep silent.   0 1 2 3 4 5

16. I am aware of nonverbal communication.   0 1 2 3 4 5

17. I am a continuous learner.   0 1 2 3 4 5

18. I empathize with members of the group.   0 1 2 3 4 5

19. I do not do anything for members of the group that they can do for themselves.   0 1 2 3 4 5

20. I am sensitive to ways members of the group relate to me as a person.　0　1　2　3　4　5

21. I am person-oriented rather than thing- or event-oriented.　0　1　2　3　4　5

22. I am meaning-oriented rather than exclusively fact-oriented.　0　1　2　3　4　5

23. I look for causes of behavior.　0　1　2　3　4　5

24. I regard each person as a person of worth.　0　1　2　3　4　5

25. I am willing to risk.　0　1　2　3　4　5

26. I constantly evaluate myself and others in the group.　0　1　2　3　4　5

27. I lead the members to think, to reach their own conclusions, to make and carry out plans.　0　1　2　3　4　5

28. I use a variety of ways of teaching which are appropriate to the goals.　0　1　2　3　4　5

29. I spend time on preparation which is commensurate with the importance of the work.　0　1　2　3　4　5

30. I am so keenly interested in my work that my enthusiasm is contagious.　0　1　2　3　4　5

31. I am continually trying to improve my personality and to be more Christlike.　0　1　2　3　4　5

32. I continually strive to improve my teaching by

   a. Observing good teachers at work.　0　1　2　3　4　5

   b. Attending meetings that assist me to do my task more effectively.　0　1　2　3　4　5

   c. Attending laboratory schools, demonstration days, and other leader development experiences.　0　1　2　3　4　5

   d. Seeking advice from experienced teachers and supervisors.　0　1　2　3　4　5

   e. Reading pertinent articles in church school periodicals.　0　1　2　3　4　5

   f. Keeping informed about denominational and ecumenical programs and informing members when possible.　0　1　2　3　4　5

   g. Studying good books on theology, psychology, and education.　0　1　2　3　4　5

Appendix B

WHAT WAS ACCOMPLISHED?

Goal: To secure reaction to the progress of the session.

1. Do you think the group accomplished anything as a result of this meeting?

   Certainly did _____   Doubt if it did _____
   Probably did _____   It did not   _____

2. To what extent was there a group goal for what we did? (Circle the number which best reflects your feelings.)

6	5	4	3	2	1	0

   We knew what we wanted and how to do it.　　Enough to function　　We wandered aimlessly

3. To what extent did the group make progress toward its goal? (Circle the number which best reflects your feelings.)

6	5	4	3	2	1	0

   Felt the group made quite a bit of progress.　　Felt there was a tendency for the group to go around in circles.

4. Was there enough opportunity for discussion?

   Too much _____   Should have been more _____
   All that was needed _____   Should have been much more _____

5. How did the members assist the progress of the group? (Circle the number which best reflects your feelings.)

6	5	4	3	2	1	0

   Felt members facilitated the progress of the group.　　For some members blocked the progress of the group.

6. To what extent was the group free to express opinions honestly?

6	5	4	3	2	1	0

Felt that we
could bring up
anything we thought
might be appropriate.

Felt the group
was restricted
from bringing up
some kinds of ideas.

7. To what extent was there clarity in the discussion?

6	5	4	3	2	1	0

Kept up with
the discussion:
Felt I understood
what was going on
all the time.

Felt somewhat
lost and confused
trying to follow
the discussion and
understand others.

8. What was the general climate of the group?

Relaxed _____	Tense _____
Warm _____	Cold _____
Friendly _____	Hostile _____

9. What were the weaknesses? How could they have been improved?

10. What were the strong points?

11. What did you think was the most critical moment during this session?

12. Do you have any suggestions about how the session could have been improved?

13. Would the session have been better if some parts would have been omitted?

Certainly not _____	Probably _____
Maybe _____	Definitely _____

P.M.R. FORM B
FIVE-POINT REACTION CHART

Goal: To secure reaction to the progress of the session.

Directions: At five points during the meeting (determined by the observer, leader, or the group as a whole) each member of the group checks an appropriate item in sections A and B. The first checking will be done in column 1, the second in column 2, and so on. (The change and flow of interest and understanding can be summarized and discussed at the end of the session.)

A. At this moment how interested or personally involved are you in the topic under consideration?

	1	2	3	4	5
1. Antagonistic					
2. Annoyed					
3. Bored					
4. No feelings one way or another					
5. Interested					
6. Challenged					
7.					

B. How clearly do you understand what is being presented or discussed at this moment?

	1	2	3	4	5
1. Unintelligible					
2. Vague					
3. Not altogether clear					
4. Generally understandable					
5. Good grasp					
6. Extremely clear					

Tabulate the ratings from all sheets onto one chart and discuss the progress of the group at the various stages of discussion.

P.M.R. FORM C
EVALUATING LEADERSHIP

Goal: To receive reaction regarding the leadership.

1. How would you rate the discussion leader? (Circle the number which best describes your response.)

6	5	4	3	2	1	0
Excellent	Very fine	Good	Fair	Not so good	Poor	Very poor

2. What kind of leadership did we have today? (Circle the number which best describes your response.)

6	5	4	3	2	1	0
Everyone shared in the leadership			Got done what the leader wanted			Everyone served his own desires

3. Was there enough preparation for the meeting?

More than needed	_____	Should have been more	_____
All that was needed	_____	Should have been much more	_____

P.M.R. FORM D
PARTICIPATION REACTION FORM

Goal: To receive reactions about participation.

1. How well do you think the participants worked together? (Circle the number which best indicates your response.)

6	5	4	3	2	1	0
Very well		Fairly well		Average		poorly

2. Most of the time I felt as if we were just a collection of persons and not really working together. (Circle the number which shows how you react to this statement.)

5	4	3	2	1	0
Yes					No

3. Most of the time I felt as if we were not really being a Christian fellowship. (Circle the number which shows how you react to this statement.)

5	4	3	2	1	0
Yes					No

4. Several members were completely silent today. What do you feel the reasons might be?

Use of abstract language	_____
Fear of being manipulated	_____
Failure to define goals	_____
Fear of group criticism	_____
Fear of losing status	_____
Desire to observe rather than participate	_____
Dependence upon others	_____
Difference in backgrounds	_____
Disinterest	_____
_____	_____
_____	_____

5. Who was most helpful in holding the group together in resolving the interpersonal problems that arose? Rank all members of the group, including the leader.

1. _____
2. _____
3. _____
4. _____
5. _____
6. _____
7. _____
8. _____
9. _____
10. _____

6. How did the group members work together?

6	5	4	3	2	1	0
Felt a cooperative relationship in the group.					Felt a good deal of unhealthy competition among members of the group.	

7. How did the group members participate?

6	5	4	3	2	1	0
Felt members encouraged each other to participate freely.					Felt members in the group did not really encourage others to participate freely.	

8. The most helpful thing anyone did today was _____

9. Today we really needed someone to _____

10. Of the things people did, I tended to admire _____

11. It really hindered our progress when _____

12. I felt uncomfortable when _____

13. It gave me a comfortable feeling when _____

14. There seemed to be a communication block between me and

THE KINDS OF ROLES THAT PARTICIPANTS PLAY IN A GROUP

(Adapted from *Group Development*, Washington, D. C.: National Training Laboratories, 1961, pp. 52-55.)

FUNCTIONAL TASK ROLES

When a group is in the process of selecting and carrying out a task, these are some of the functional roles people play:

1. *Initiator*. A person who proposes tasks, goals, or solutions; one who suggests new ideas, new definitions of the problem, new attacks on the problem, or new organization of material.

2. *Information-seeker*. A person who asks for clarification of suggestions, requesting additional information or facts.

3. *Opinion-seeker*. A person who looks for an expression of feeling about something from the members, seeking clarification of values, suggestions, or ideas.

4. *Information-giver*. A person who offers facts or generalizations; one who relates his own experience to the group problem to illustrate a point; one who provides relevant information about the group concern.

5. *Opinion-giver*. A person who states an opinion or belief concerning a suggestion, particularly concerning its value rather than its factual basis.

6. *Clarifier*. A person who interprets or rewords another per-

139

P.M.R. FORM E

ROLES PLAYED BY PARTICIPANTS

Goal: To determine what roles people play in the group.
Indicate the appropriate role each time a person contributes to
the group. These roles are defined on pages 139, 141-142.

	A	B	C	D	E	F	G	H	I	J	K	L	M	N	O	P	Q
1. Initiator																	
2. Information-seeker																	
3. Opinion-seeker																	
4. Information-giver																	
5. Opinion-giver																	
6. Clarifier																	
7. Elaborator																	
8. Coordinator																	
9. Summarizer																	
10. Feasibility-tester																	
11. Listener																	
12. Encourager																	
13. Gatekeeper																	
14. Standard-setter																	
15. Compromiser																	
16. Follower																	
17. Commentator																	
18. Evaluator																	
19. Diagnostician																	
20. Consensus-tester																	
21. Harmonizer																	
22. Tension-reliever																	
23. Aggressor																	
24. Blocker																	
25. Recognition-seeker																	
26. Self-confessor																	
27. Playboy																	
28. Dominator																	
29. Help-seeker																	
30. Special-interest pleader																	

son's contributions to determine if the meaning is really understood; one who attempts to clear up confusions.

7. *Elaborator.* A person who develops meanings or gives examples.

8. *Coordinator.* A person who shows relationships among various ideas or suggestions; one who tries to pull ideas and suggestions together; one who tries to draw together activities of various subgroups or members.

9. *Summarizer.* A person who restates suggestions after the group has discussed them.

10. *Feasibility-tester.* A person who examines the practicality and workability of ideas; one who preevaluates decisions.

FUNCTIONAL GROUP-BUILDING AND MAINTENANCE ROLES

Although a group may have a task to select and to carry out, it is important to strengthen and maintain group life. The roles listed below aid in effective group growth and production.

11. *Listener.* A person who actively listens to the contributions of others and does not participate in fringe conversations.

12. *Encourager.* A person who is friendly, warm, and responsive to others; one who praises others and their ideas; one who agrees with and accepts contributions of others; one who builds upon other persons' contributions.

13. *Gatekeeper.* A person who attempts to keep communication channels open; one who facilitates the participation of others; one who tries to regulate the flow of communication; one who keeps a minority view before the group.

14. *Standard-setter.* A person who suggests standards for the group to use in choosing its content or procedures; one who suggests standards for evaluating its decisions or the quality of the group process.

15. *Compromiser.* A person who offers to compromise his own position when his own idea or status is involved; one who disciplines himself to maintain group harmony; one who admits his error.

16. *Follower.* A person who goes along with decisions of the group, somewhat passively accepting the ideas of others; one who serves as an audience during group discussion or group decision-making.

17. *Commentator.* A person who summarizes what the group feeling is sensed to be; one who describes the reactions of the group to ideas, solutions, or to other group members.

FUNCTIONAL TASK AND GROUP-BUILDING ROLES

Some functions serve to assist in achieving the accomplishment of a task as well as developing group worth.

18. *Evaluator.* A person who compares group decisions or accomplishments with the group goals.

19. *Diagnostician.* A person who determines the sources of difficulties; one who suggests appropriate steps to take next.

20. *Consensus-tester.* A person who tentatively asks for group opinions in order to find out if the group is nearing consensus on a decision.

21. *Harmonizer.* A person who mediates differences between other members; one who attempts to reconcile disagreements.

22. *Tension-reliever.* A person who jests or pours oil on troubled waters to relieve tensions; one who puts a tense situation in a wider context.

NONFUNCTIONAL ROLES

Roles which concentrate on self-centeredness deter group growth and the accomplishment of the group's task.

23. *Aggressor.* A person who attacks openly what another person has said or the task at hand; one who violates the rights of others; one who shows envy toward another person's contribution by taking credit for it.

24. *Blocker.* A person who reacts unfavorably to everything the group members want to do; one who gripes a lot and seldom says anything constructive; one who raises the same personal issues or refers every matter back to his same personal problems; one whose comments are not relevant.

25. *Recognition-seeker.* A person who continually calls attention to himself; one who boasts about his personal achievements.

26. *Self-confessor.* A person who expresses his own personal feelings or insights that are not related to the group's task.

27. *Playboy.* A person who outwardly shows his disinterest in the group's process or task; one who is cynical, nonchalant, or who participates in horseplay.

28. *Dominator.* A person who asserts his authority by manipulating others; one who interrupts the contributions of others; one who talks too much.

29. *Help-seeker.* A person who calls for sympathy from the group members; one who depreciates himself beyond reason.

30. *Special-interest pleader.* A person who pleads for special areas of emphasis or stereotypes and who usually cloaks his own prejudices in the stereotype that best fits.

P.M.R. FORM F
WHAT HAPPENED?

Goal: To receive a general reaction to the session.

1. How did you approach the discussion? (Circle the number which best shows your response.)

6	5	4	3	2	1	0
With expectation						With indifference

2. How did you like today's session? (Circle the appropriate number.)

6	5	4	3	2	1	0
Excellent	Very fine	Good	Fair	Not so good	Poor	Very poor

3. Rate the value of the event to you. (Circle the appropriate number.)

5	4	3	2	1	0
Excellent	Good	Fair	Poor	Very poor	Harmful

What specific experience, interaction, encounter, conversation, happening, feeling during the event most influenced the rating above?

4. Were you interested in the topic? (Circle the appropriate number.)

6	5	4	3	2	1	0
Very much		Quite a bit		Not much		Not at all

5. Did you talk about some ideas that were really exciting and important? (Circle the appropriate number.)

5	4	3	2	1	0
Yes					No

6. What did you like best?

7. What did you like least?

8. What will be most useful to you?

9. What surprised you most?

10. What disappointed you most?

11. How did you feel about the tempo of the meeting?

12. How clearly did your goals coincide with the group goals? (Circle the appropriate number.)

6	5	4	3	2	1	0
Identical		Somewhat similar		Somewhat different		Not at all

13. In what ways were you helped spiritually?

14. What was the meaning of this time together?

15. What did you learn about yourself today?

16. What suggestions do you have for the next session?

P.M.R. FORM G
INFORMATION REACTION FORM

Goal: To secure a reaction about information received.

1. What was the depth of our discussion? (Circle the appropriate number.)

6	5	4	3	2	1	0
Very deep			Occasionally deep			Shallow, flighty

2. Did you gain any new ideas or concepts from the discussion? (Circle the appropriate number.)

6	5	4	3	2	1	0
Many	Quite a few	Several	Some	Not many	Few	None

3. Did the discussion help clarify any problems? It was

Very helpful _____   Of some help _____   Not too helpful _____   Useless _____

4. I gained the following new ideas:

5. What conclusions have you reached as a result of this session?

6. What do you think should be dealt with more adequately?

7. What specific things would you personally like to spend additional time to explore or to try out?

P.M.R. FORM H
WAS THERE CHANGE?

Goal: To receive reaction about change.

1. Did you have a firm opinion about the topic before the session?

Yes _____   No _____

2. How did you feel about a possible change in your position? (Circle the appropriate number.)

5	4	3	2	1	0
Open to change					Closed to change

3. Did you change your opinion in any way during the discussion? (Circle the appropriate number.)

5	4	3	2	1	0
Completely changed					No change

4. Were your opinions confirmed or strengthened?

Very much _____   Some but not much _____   None _____
Quite a bit _____   Very little   _____

5. In what ways do you plan to use these new ideas?

P.M.R. FORM I
MY PARTICIPATION

Goal: To receive reaction about a person's participation.

1. How did you feel as a member of the group? (Circle the number which reflects your feelings.)

5	4	3	2	1	0
Felt really in the group					Felt like an outsider to the group

2. How did others receive your contributions? (Circle the appropriate number.)

6	5	4	3	2	1	0
Well received			Some responded favorably			Brushed off; disregarded

3. How did you try to understand the contributions of others? (Circle the appropriate number.)

6	5	4	3	2	1	0
Tried my best to understand		Mildly interested		Defensive		Not interested; I had the truth

4. How did you help the discussion?

5. How did you hinder the discussion?

6. Did you find yourself wanting to say things that you didn't actually say? (Circle the appropriate number.)

4	3	2	1	0
Very frequently	Frequently	Fairly often	A few times	Never

7. Were there any reasons why you did not contribute? If so, list them.

8. How free were you to tell your real opinions and feelings?

Very free _____   Free _____   So-so _____   Not free _____

9. I was able to share a conviction I really felt deeply about. (Circle the appropriate number.)

5	4	3	2	1	0
Yes					No

10. There were times when I really felt as if I were being understood and being helped to say what I wanted to say. (Circle the appropriate number.)

5	4	3	2	1	0
Yes					No

11. How much am I being honest and frank? (Circle the appropriate number.)

6	5	4	3	2	1	0
Most of the time; whenever appropriate			Sometimes, but not always			Very little; can't let myself loose

12. I felt that I did not do a very good job at _____

13. I had a feeling of accomplishment when I _____

14. I feel that I would like to change the way in which I _____

P.M.R. FORM J
PERSONAL GROWTH CHART *

Goal: To receive reaction of personal growth.

In your opinion, have you grown in your ability to work with others as a responsible member of a learning team? Put a check at the appropriate place for each item.

	Much Growth	Little Growth	No Growth	Un-certain	Previously achieved
1. Assisting others to participate.					
2. Sharing my opinions and ideas with others.					
3. Actively facing conflicts which arise in the group.					
4. Helping resolve problem situations rather than depending entirely on the leader.					
5. Asking for clarification when I do not understand something.					
6. Sometimes restating others' contributions for personal clarification.					
7. Listening to others attentively.					
8. Being frank in expressing ideas and opinions.					
9. Trying to help others with their problems of understanding.					
10. Asking for help.					
11. Sharing the blame for poor teamwork.					
12. Being less defensive.					
13. Relying less on the leader for direction.					

	Much Growth	Little Growth	No Growth	Un-certain	Previously achieved
14. Having ability to recognize my real needs.					
15. Trying to translate what I learn into action.					
16. Keeping the minority view before the group.					
17. Not belittling others for their lack of understanding.					
18. Accepting other participants as individuals when I disagree with their ideas.					
19. Being willing to risk myself.					

* Adapted from a mimeographed form entitled "Appraisal of Personal Growth in Teamwork" prepared by the Bureau of Studies in Adult Education, Indiana University, Bloomington, Indiana.

Notes

CHAPTER 1

[1] Edward Friedenberg, *The Vanishing Adolescent* (New York: Dell Publishing Co., 1959).

[2] Gale Jensen; A. A. Liveright; and Wilbur Hallenbeck, *Adult Education* (Washington, D.C.: Adult Education Association of the U.S.A., 1964), p. 28.

[3] Reuel L. Howe, *The Creative Years* (New York: The Seabury Press, Inc., 1964), pp. 197-209; Will Menninger, "The Criteria of Emotional Maturity"; H. A. Overstreet, *The Mature Mind* (New York: W. N. Norton & Co., 1959), pp. 42-71; Robert A. Dow, "Small Group Leadership," (Green Lake, Wis.: American Baptist Assembly, 1969. Multilithed); *Perceiving, Behaving, Becoming, A New Focus for Education* (Washington, D.C.: Association for Supervision and Curriculum Development, 1962), pp. 17-20.

[4] Earl F. Zeigler, *Christian Education of Adults* (Philadelphia: The Westminster Press, 1958), pp. 87-129.

CHAPTER 2

[1] Ralph W. Tyler, *Basic Principles of Curriculum and Instruction* (Chicago: The University of Chicago Press, 1950), p. 41.

[2] Calvin E. Harbin, *Teaching Power* (New York: Philosophical Library, 1967), pp. 29-30.

CHAPTER 3

[1] Ralph W. Tyler, *Basic Principles of Curriculum and Instruction* (Chicago: The University of Chicago Press, 1950), p. 41.

[2] D. Campbell Wyckoff, *Learning Tasks in the Curriculum,* Edited and published by the Department of Curriculum Research and Development (Valley Forge: American Baptist Board of Education and Publication, 1965), pp. 12-16.

[3] Charles R. Stinette, Jr., *Learning in Theological Perspective* (New York: Association Press, 1965), p. 68.

[4] Benjamin S. Bloom, ed., *Taxonomy of Educational Objectives. Handbook 1: Cognitive Domain* (New York: Longmans, Green and Co., 1956), pp. 7ff. Bloom and his associates call these the cognitive (knowing), the affective (feeling), and the psychomatic (doing) levels.

[5] David Krathwohl; Benjamin S. Bloom; and Bertram B. Masia, *Taxonomy of Educational Objectives. Handbook 2: Affective Domain* (New York: David McKay Co., Inc., 1964), pp. 49-50.

[6] Ross Snyder, *On Becoming Human*, (Nashville: Abingdon Press, 1967), pp. 27-31.

[7] Kurt Lewin, "Group Decision and Social Change," *Readings in Social Psychology*, ed. Theodore M. Newcomb and Eugene L. Hartley (New York: Holt, Rinehart & Winston, Inc., 1947), pp. 330-344.

[8] George B. Leonard, *Education and Ecstasy* (New York: The Delacorte Press, 1968), p. 20.

CHAPTER 4

[1] D. Campbell Wyckoff, *Learning Tasks in the Curriculum*, Edited and published by the Department of Curriculum Research and Development (Valley Forge: American Baptist Board of Education and Publication, 1965), p. 13.

CHAPTER 7

[1] D. Campbell Wyckoff, *Learning Tasks in the Curriculum*, Edited and published by the Department of Curriculum Research and Development (Valley Forge: American Baptist Board of Education and Publication, 1965), pp. 15-16.

CHAPTER 8

[1] Leland P. Bradford, ed., *Human Forces in Teaching and Learning* (Washington, D.C.: National Training Laboratories, 1961), p. 53.

[2] Ross Snyder, *On Becoming Human* (Nashville: Abingdon Press, 1967), p. 4.

[3] Philip A. Anderson, *Church Meetings that Matter* (Philadelphia: United Church Press, 1965), pp. 94-103.

CHAPTER 9

[1] Horace M. Kallen, *Philosophical Issues in Adult Education* (Springfield, Ill.: Charles C. Thomas, Publisher, 1962), p. 43.

CHAPTER 11

[1] *Foundations for Curriculum* (Valley Forge: American Baptist Board of Education and Publication, 1966), p. 44.

[2] Nathan W. Turner, "The Elective Principle," *The Torch*, vol. 10, no. 4, p. 4.

[3] Carolyn Goddard, "The Wheel: A Model for Multi-Media Learning," *Colloquy*, vol. 2, no. 7, pp. 38-41. Miss Goddard bases her interpretation on Murray Suid; Roberta Suid; and James Morrow, "The Wheel: A Model for Multi-Media Learning," *Educators Guide to Media and Methods*, vol. 5, no. 1, pp. 29-33.

CHAPTER 12

[1] Paul Bergevin and Dwight Morris, *A Manual for Group Discussion Participants* (New York: The Seabury Press, Inc., 1965). A good resource for this procedure.

[2] John L. Casteel, ed., *The Creative Role of Interpersonal Groups in the Church Today* (New York: Association Press, 1968), pp. 172-187; Paul Bergevin and John McKinley, *Participation Training for Adult Education* (St. Louis: Bethany Press, 1967). Also, see Robert A. Dow, *Learning Through Encounter* (Valley Forge: Judson Press, 1971).

[3] Edgar H. Schein and Warren G. Bennis, *Personal and Organizational Change Through Group Methods* (New York: John Wiley & Sons, Inc., 1965).

[4] *Encountertapes for Personal Growth Groups*, developed by Betty Berzon and Jerome Reisel at The Western Behaviorial Sciences Institute, La Jolla, California.

[5] Richard R. Broholm, *Strategic Planning for Church Organizations* (Valley Forge: Judson Press, 1969).

Bibliography

(Books which are marked with * are basic books for the subject.)

GENERAL BOOKS

Anderson, Phoebe M., *Living and Learning in the Church School*. Philadelphia: United Church Press, 1965.

*Ashbrook, James, *be/come Community*. Valley Forge: Judson Press, 1970.

Becker Edwin L., *Responding to God's Call*. St. Louis: Bethany Press, 1970.

Ferre, Nels F., *A Theology for Christian Education*. Philadelphia: The Westminster Press, 1967.

Foundations for Curriculum. Valley Forge: American Baptist Board of Education and Publication, 1966. (Multilithed.)

*Hazelton, Roger, *Knowing the Living God*. Valley Forge: Judson Press, 1969.

*Hunter, David R., *Christian Education as Engagement*. New York: The Seabury Press, Inc., 1963.

LeBar, Lois Emogene, *Education that Is Christian*. Westwood, N. J.: Fleming H. Revell Co., 1958.

Leypoldt, Martha M., "An Analysis of Seminary Courses Specifically Designed to Prepare Seminary Students to Assist Adults toward Christian Maturity through the Adult Education Program of a Local Church." Unpublished doctor's dissertation, School of Education, Indiana University, 1964.

Marty, Martin E., *The Search for a Usable Future*. New York: Harper & Row, Publishers, 1969.

Minor, Harold D., *New Ways for a New Day*. Nashville: Abingdon Press, 1965.

*Russell, Letty M., *Christian Education in Mission*. Philadelphia: The Westminster Press, 1967.

*Stagg, Paul L., *The Converted Church*. Valley Forge: Judson Press, 1967.

Tibbetts, Orlando L., *The Reconciling Community*. Valley Forge: Judson Press, 1969.

Turner, Nathan W., "The Elective Principle," *The Torch*, vol. 10, no. 4 (July, 1969), pp. 4-5.

Tyler, Ralph W., *Basic Principles of Curriculum and Instruction*. Chicago: The University of Chicago Press, 1950.

Wyckoff, D. Campbell, *Theory and Design of Christian Education Curriculum*. Philadelphia: The Westminster Press, 1961.

CREATIVITY

Osborn, Alex F., *Applied Imagination*, rev. ed. New York: Charles Scribner's Sons, 1963.

Parnes, Sidney J., *Creative Behavior Guidebook*. New York: Charles Scribner's Sons, 1967.

_____, *Creative Behavior Workbook*. New York: Charles Scribner's Sons, 1967.

Parnes, Sidney J., and Harding, Harold F., eds., *A Source Book for Creative Thinking*. New York: Charles Scribner's Sons, 1962.

Weschler, Irving W., *The Leader and Creativity*. New York: Association Press, 1962.

INTERPERSONAL RELATIONSHIPS IN SMALL GROUPS

*Anderson, Philip A., *Church Meetings that Matter*. Philadelphia: United Church Press, 1965.

Bergevin, Paul, and McKinley, John, *Participation Training for Adult Education*. St. Louis: Bethany Press, 1967.

Bergevin, Paul, and Morris, Dwight, *A Manual for Group Discussion Participants*. New York: The Seabury Press, Inc., 1965.

Bradford, Leland P., ed., *Human Forces in Teaching and Learning*. Washington, D.C.: National Training Laboratories, 1961.

Burton, Arthur, ed., *Encounter*. San Francisco: Jossey-Bass, Inc., Publishers, 1970.

Casteel, John L., ed., *The Creative Role of Interpersonal Groups in the Church Today*. New York: Association Press, 1968.

*Day, LeRoy Judson, *Dynamic Christian Fellowship*, rev. ed. Valley Forge: Judson Press, 1962.

Foster, Virgil E., "Teaching in the Midst of Controversy," *International Journal of Religious Education*, vol. 44, no. 5 (January, 1968), pp. 3, 4, 27.

General Relationship Improvement Program. (A programmed course designed to improve relations and aid creativity between two people.) Atlanta, Georgia: Human Development Institute, 1967.

Gibb, Jack R.; Platts, Grace N.; and Miller, Lorraine F., *Dynamics of Participative Groups*. Washington, D.C.: National Training Laboratories, 1951.

*Howe, Reuel L., *The Miracle of Dialogue*. New York: The Seabury Press, Inc., 1963.

Little, Sara, *Learning Together in the Christian Fellowship*. Richmond: John Knox Press, 1956.

Maier, Norman R., *Problem-Solving Discussions and Conferences*. New York: McGraw-Hill Book Company, Inc., 1963.

Middleman, Ruth R., *The Non-Verbal Method in Working with Groups*. New York: Association Press, 1968.

Miles, Matthew B., *Learning to Work in Groups*. New York: Bureau of Publications, Teachers College Press, Columbia University, 1959.

Mills, Theodore M., *The Sociology of Small Groups*. Englewood Cliffs, N. J.: Prentice-Hall, Inc., 1967.

*Peterson, Miriam, *The Role of Small Groups and Group Leadership in the Church's Ministry*. Valley Forge: Judson Press, n.d.

Rogers, Carl R., *Carl Rogers on Encounter Groups*, New York: Harper & Row, Publishers, 1970.

Schein, Edgar H., and Bennis, Warren G., *Personal and Organizational Change through Group Methods: The Laboratory Approach*. New York: John Wiley & Sons, Inc., 1965.

Schutz, William C., *Joy: Expanding Human Awareness*. New York: Grove Press 1967.

Smith, Henry Clay, *Sensitivity to People*. New York: McGraw-Hill Book Company, 1966.

Team Style Diagnosis Test (Contains one large chart and ten individual criterion charts). Fredericton, New Brunswick, Canada: Managerial Effectiveness Ltd., 1967.

Watson, G., ed., *Group Development*. Washington, D.C.: National Training Laboratories, 1961.

Weschler, Irving W., and Schein, Edgar H., eds., *Issues in Human Relations Training*. Washington, D.C.: National Training Laboratories, 1962.

LEADERSHIP IN SMALL GROUPS

Buchanan, Paul C., *The Leader and Individual Motivation*. New York: Association Press, 1963.

Lippitt, Gordon L., ed., *Leadership in Action*. Washington, D.C.: National Training Laboratories, 1961.

Lippitt, Gordon L., and Seashore, Edith, *The Leader and Group Effectiveness*. New York: Association Press, 1962.

Liveright, A. A., *Strategies of Leadership in Conducting Adult Education Programs*. New York: Harper & Row, Publishers, 1959.

MEDIA

Abbey, Merrill R., *Man, Media and the Message*. New York: Friendship Press, 1970.

Andersen, Robert W., and Caemmerer, Richard R., Jr., *Banners, Etc.* Chicago: Christian Art Associates, 1967.

Dalglish, William A., ed., *Media for Christian Formation*. Dayton, Ohio: George A. Pflaum, Pub., Inc., 1969.

Encountertapes for Personal Growth Groups. (A program of interpersonal exercises for small self-directed groups.) Developed by Betty Berzon and Jerome Reisel at The Western Behaviorial Sciences Institute, La Jolla, California.

Fore, William F., *Image and Impact*. New York: Friendship Press, 1970.

Goddard, Carolyn, "The Wheel: A Model for Multi-Media Learning," *Colloquy*, vol. 2, no. 7 (July-August, 1969), pp. 38-41.

Hall, Cameron P., *Human Values and Advancing Technology*. New York: Friendship Press, 1967.

Heyer, Robert, and Meyer, Anthony, *Discovery in Film*. New York: Association Press, 1969.

Jackson, B. F., Jr., ed., *Communication for Churchmen*. Vol. 2, *Television—Radio—Film for Churchmen*. Nashville: Abingdon Press, 1969.

_____, *Communication for Churchmen*. Vol. 3, *Audiovisual Facilities and Equipment for Churchmen*, Nashville: Abingdon Press, 1970.

Jones, G. William, *Sunday Night at the Movies*. Richmond: John Knox Press, 1967.

McLuhan, Marshall, *Understanding Media*. New York: The New American Library, 1964.

Ohlinger, John, *The Mass Media in Adult Education: A Review of Recent Literature*. Syracuse: ERIC Clearinghouse on Adult Education, 1968.

Rossi, Peter H., and Biddle, Bruce J., eds., *The New Media and Education*. Chicago: Aldine Publishing Company, 1966.

Suid, Murray; Suid, Roberta; and Morrow, James, "The Wheel: A Model for Multi-Media Learning," *Educators Guide to Media and Methods*, vol. 5, no. 1 (September, 1968), pp. 29-33.

Woods, Richard, *The Media Maze*. Dayton, Ohio: George A. Pflaum, 1969.

MULTI-MEDIA KITS

Creative Arts in Reconciliation. (Contains a book, filmstrips, and a record.) New York: Friendship Press, 1969.

Creative Problem Solving for Commitees on Christian Education. (Contains Participant's Books, 3 cassettes, and 6 posters.) Philadelphia: Lutheran Church Press, 1970.

Harrell, John and Mary. *Communicating the Gospel Today*. (Contains several small books and a candle.) Berkeley, Calif.: John and Mary Harrell, 1968.

_____, *Time Being*. (A Happening for Christians Alive.) Berkeley, Calif.: John and Mary Harrell, 1970.

Kent, Sister Mary Corita; Cox, Harvey; and Eisenstein, Samuel A., *Sister Corita*. (Contains a book with many prints, a banner, and a set of single pictures for mounting.) Philadelphia: Pilgrim Press, n.d.

OBJECTIVES

Bloom, Benjamin S., ed., *Taxonomy of Educational Objectives, Handbook I: Cognitive Domain.* New York: Longmans, Green and Co., 1956.

Krathwohl, David R.; Bloom, Benjamin S.; and Mesia, Bertram B., *Taxonomy of Educational Objectives, Handbook II: Affective Domain.* New York: David McKay Co., Inc., 1964.

*Mager, Robert F., *Preparing Instructional Objectives.* Palo Alto: Fearon Publishers, 1962.

PLANNING

*Broholm, Richard R., *Strategic Planning for Church Organizations.* Valley Forge: Judson Press, 1969.

McKinley, John, and Smith, Robert M., *Guide to Program Planning.* New York: The Seabury Press, Inc., 1965.

PSYCHOLOGY AND HUMAN DEVELOPMENT

Bernard, Harold W., and Huckins, Wesley C., *Readings in Educational Psychology.* Scranton, Pa.: International Textbook Co., 1967.

Birren, James E., *The Psychology of Aging.* Englewood Cliffs, N. J.: Prentice-Hall, Inc., 1964.

Brighter Vistas: Church Programs for Older Adults. Washington, D.C.: U.S. Department of Health, Education and Welfare Administration on Aging, 1965.

Cronbach, Lee J., *Educational Psychology,* 2nd ed. New York: Harcourt, Brace, Jovanovich, Inc., 1963.

Doniger, Simon L., ed., *Becoming the Complete Adult.* New York: Association Press, 1962.

Erikson, Erik H., *Childhood and Society,* rev. ed. New York: W. W. Norton and Company, Inc., 1968.

Franklin, Lottie M., *So You Work with Young Adults.* Anderson, Ind.: Warner Press, 1960.

Friedenberg, Edgar Z., *The Vanishing Adolescent.* New York: Dell Publishing Co., Inc., 1962.

Havighurst, Robert J., *Human Development and Education.* New York: Longmans, Green and Co., 1953.

Howe, Reuel L., *The Creative Years.* New York: The Seabury Press, Inc., 1964.

Klein, Wilma H.; LeShan, Eda J.; and Furman, Sylvan S., *Promoting Mental Health of Older People through Group Methods.* New York: Mental Health Materials Center, 1965.

Larsen, Dorothy Hill, *Dialogues on Aging.* New York: Teachers College Press, Columbia University, 1966.

Moore, Allen J., *The Young Adult Generation.* Nashville: Abingdon Press, 1969.

Newcomb, Theodore, and Hartley, Eugene, eds., *Readings in Social Psychology.* New York: Holt, Rinehart & Winston, Inc., 1947.

Peterson, Miriam A., *The Church's Ministry with Senior Adults.* Valley Forge: The Department of Ministry with Adults, American Baptist Board of Education and Publication, 1966.

Pressey, Sidney L.; Robinson, Francis P.; and Horrocks, John E., *Psychology in Education.* New York: Harper & Row, Publishers, 1959.

Robb, Thomas Bradley, *The Bonus Years.* Valley Forge: Judson Press, 1968.

Sherrill, Lewis J., *The Struggle of the Soul.* New York: The Macmillan Company, 1951.

SELF-RENEWAL

Allport, Gordon W., *Becoming*. New Haven: Yale University Press, 1955.

_____, *The Person in Psychology*. Boston: Beacon Press, 1968.

Berne, Eric, *Games People Play*. New York: Grove Press, Inc., 1964.

Fosdick, Harry Emerson, *On Being a Real Person*. New York: Harper & Row, Publishers, 1943.

Fromm, Erich, *The Art of Loving*. New York: Harper & Row, Publishers, 1956.

*Gardner, John W., *Self-Renewal*. New York: Harper & Row, Publishers, 1964.

Hites, Robert W., *The Act of Becoming*. Nashville: Abingdon Press, 1965.

*Howe, Reuel L., *Herein Is Love*. Valley Forge: Judson Press, 1961.

Jourard, Sidney M., *The Transparent Self*. Princeton: D. Van Nostrand Co., Inc., 1964.

Leeper, Robert R., ed., *Humanizing Education: The Person in the Process*. Washington, D.C.: Association for Supervision and Curriculum Development, 1967.

Maslow, Abraham H., *Toward a Psychology of Being*. Princeton: D. Van Nostrand Co., Inc., 1962.

O'Connor, Elizabeth, *Our Many Selves*. New York: Harper & Row, Publishers, 1971.

Overstreet, H. A., *The Mature Mind*. New York: W. W. Norton & Company, Inc., 1949.

Perceiving—Behaving—Becoming. Washington, D.C.: Association for Supervision and Curriculum Development,, 1962.

Rogers, Carl R., *On Becoming a Person*. Boston: Houghton Mifflin Company, 1961.

Shostrom, Everett L., *Man, the Manipulator*. Nashville: Abingdon Press, 1967.

*Snyder, Ross, *On Becoming Human*. Nashville: Abingdon Press, 1967.

Tournier, Paul, *Secrets*. Richmond, Va.: John Knox Press, 1965.

_____, *To Resist or To Surrender*. Richmond, Va.: John Knox Press, 1964.

_____, *To Understand Each Other*. Richmond, Va.: John Knox Press, 1967.

TEACHING AND LEARNING

*Ban, Joseph D., *Education for Change*. Valley Forge: Judson Press, 1968.

Bergevin, Paul, *A Philosophy for Adult Education*. New York: The Seabury Press, Inc., 1967.

Bigge, Morris L., *Learning Theories for Teachers*. New York: Harper & Row, Publishers, 1964.

*Bowman, Locke E., Jr., *Straight Talk about Teaching in Today's Church*. Philadelphia: The Westminster Press, 1967.

Bruner, Jerome S., *The Process of Education*. New York: Random House, Inc., 1960.

Clemmons, Robert S., *Education for Churchmanship*. Nashville: Abingdon Press, 1966.

Dow, Robert A., *Learning through Encounter*. Valley Forge: Judson Press, 1971.

Ensley, Gerald F., *Persons Can Change*. Nashville: Abingdon Press, 1964.

Foster, Virgil E., *Christian Education Where the Learning Is*. Englewood Cliffs, N. J.: Prentice-Hall, Inc., 1968.

Good, Carter V., *Dictionary of Education*, 2nd ed. New York: McGraw-Hill Book Company, 1959.

Harbin, Calvin E., *Teaching Power*. New York: Philosophical Library, 1967.

Henry, Nelson B., ed., *Adult Reading*. The Fifty-fifth Yearbook of the National Society for the Study of Education, Part II. Chicago: The University of Chicago Press, 1956.

——————, *The Dynamics of Instructional Groups*. The Fifty-ninth Yearbook of the National Society for the Study of Education. Part II. Chicago: The University of Chicago Press, 1960.

Hilgard, Ernest R., *Theories of Learning*. The Sixty-third Yearbook of the National Society for the Study of Education, Part I. Chicago: The University of Chicago Press, 1964.

Hilgard, Ernest R., and Bower, Gordon H., *Theories of Learning*, 3rd ed. Appleton-Century-Crofts, 1966.

Hotchkiss, Lois E., "How Some Adults Learn How to Teach," *Adult Leadership*, vol. 18, no. 2 (June, 1969), pp. 47, 48, 54, 66.

Houle, Cyril O., *Continuing Your Education*. New York: McGraw-Hill Book Company, 1964.

——————, *The Inquiring Mind*. Madison: The University of Wisconsin Press, 1961.

Jackson, B. F., Jr., ed., *Communication: Learning for Churchmen*, vol. I. Nashville: Abingdon Press, 1968.

Jensen, Gale; Liveright, A. A.; and Hallenbeck, Wilbur, *Adult Education*. Washington, D.C.: Adult Education Association of the U.S.A., 1964.

Kallen, Horace M., *Philosophical Issues in Adult Education*. Springfield, Ill.: Charles C. Thomas, Publisher, 1962.

Kerr, John Stevens, *Happiness is a Teacher*. Philadelphia: Lutheran Church Press, 1967.

Kidd, J. R., *How Adults Learn*. New York: Association Press, 1959.

Knowles, Malcolm S., *The Modern Practice of Adult Education*. New York: Association Press, 1970.

Learning Tasks in the Curriculum. Valley Forge: American Baptist Board of Education and Publication, 1965. (Multilithed.)

Leonard, George B., *Education and Ecstasy*. New York: The Delacorte Press, 1968.

Leypoldt, Martha M., "The Teaching—Learning Process with Adults," *Adult Leadership*, vol. 16, no. 6 (December, 1967), pp. 212, 213, 233.

Mager, Robert F., *Developing Attitude Toward Learning*. Palo Alto: Fearon Publishers, Inc., 1968.

Maves, Paul B., *Understanding Ourselves as Adults*. Nashville; Abingdon Press, 1959.

Merjanian, Pepronia, *The Joy of Teaching*. Philadelphia: United Church Press, 1966.

Miller, Harry L., *Teaching and Learning in Adult Education*. New York: The Macmillan Company, 1964.

Miller, Harry L., and McGuire, Christine, *Evaluating Liberal Adult Education*. Chicago: The Center for the Study of Liberal Education for Adults, 1961.

Miller, T. Franklin *et. al.*, *Basics for Teaching in the Church*. Anderson, Ind.: Warner Press, Inc., 1968.

Morphet, Edgar L., and Ryan, Charles O., eds., *Designing Education for the Future, No. 2, Implications for Education of Prospective Changes in Society*. New York: Citation Press, 1967.

——————, *Designing Education for the Future, No. 3, Effecting Needed Changes in Education*. New York: Citation Press, 1967.

Pfnister, Allan O., *Teaching Adults*. Philadelphia: United Church Press, 1967.

Riday, George E., *Understanding the Learner*. Valley Forge: Judson Press, 1964.

Rood, Wayne R., *The Art of Teaching Christianity*. Nashville: Abingdon Press, 1968.

Simpson, Ray H., *Teacher Self-Evaluation*. New York: The Macmillan Company, 1966.

Stinnette, Charles R., Jr., *Learning in Theological Perspective*. New York: Association Press, 1965.

Swain, Dorothy G., *Teach Me to Teach*. Valley Forge: Judson Press, 1964.

Verner, Coolie, and Booth, Alan, *Adult Education*. Washington, D.C.: The Center for Applied Research in Education, Inc., 1964.

Verner, Coolie; Lorge, Irving; and White, Thurman, eds., *Adult Learning*. Washington, D.C.: Adult Education Association of the U.S.A., 1965.

Verner, Coolie; Miller, Henry L.; and Booth, Alan, *Processes of Adult Education*. Washington, D.C.: Adult Education Association of the U.S.A., 1965.

Zeigler, Earl F., *Christian Education of Adults*. Philadelphia: The Westminster Press, 1958.

Ziegler, Jesse H., *Focus on Adults*. Elgin, Ill.: The Brethren Press, 1965.

TEAM TEACHING

Anderson, Frances M., *Team Teaching in Christian Education*. Chicago: Evangelical Covenant Church of America, 1967.

*Holcomb, Jerry, *Team Teaching with the Scotts and Bartons*. Valley Forge: Judson Press, 1968.

Polos, Nicholas C., *The Dynamics of Team Teaching*. Dubuque: William C. Brown Company, Publishers, 1965.

TECHNIQUES OF TEACHING

Bergevin, Paul; Morris, Dwight; and Smith, Robert M., *Adult Education Procedures*. New York: The Seabury Press, Inc., 1963.

Boocock, Sarane S. and Schild, E. O., eds., *Simulation Games in Learning*. Beverly Hills: Sage Publications, Inc., 1968.

Bormann, Ernest G., *Workbook for Work Groups*. Minneapolis: Gordon Press, 1966. (Mimeographed.)

Brown, Helen A., and Heltman, Harry, Jr., eds., *Choral Readings from the Bible*. Philadelphia: The Westminster Press, 1955.

_____, *Choral Reading for Worship and Inspiration*. Philadelphia: The Westminster Press, 1954.

Can of Squirms: A New Approach to Role-playing. (Separate cans for college age and adults. Contains role-playing situations and leader's guide.) Downers Grove, Ill.: Contemporary Drama Service, n.d.

Davis, Morton D., *Game Theory*. New York: Basic Books, Inc., 1970.

Klein, Alan F., *Role-Playing in Leadership Training and Group Problem Solving*. New York: Association Press, 1956.

Levit, Grace, and Jennings, Helen, *How to Use Role Playing*. Washington, D.C.: Adult Education Association of the U.S.A., 1956.

*Leypoldt, Martha M., *40 Ways to Teach in Groups*. Valley Forge: Judson Press, 1967.

McKinley, John, *Creative Methods for Adult Classes*. St. Louis: Bethany Press, 1960.

Minor, Harold D., *Creative Procedures for Adult Groups*. Nashville: Abingdon Press, 1968.

Morgan, Barton; Holmes, Glenn E.; and Bundy, Clarence E., *Methods in Adult Education*, 2nd ed. Danville, Ill.: The Interstate Printers and Publishers, Inc., 1963.

Morrison, Eleanor S., and Foster, Virgil E., *Creative Teaching in the Church*. Englewood Cliffs, N. J.: Prentice-Hall, Inc., 1963.

Nylen, Donald J.; Mitchell, J. Robert; and Stout, Anthony, *Handbook of Staff Development and Human Relations Training: Materials Developed for Use in Africa,* rev. and expanded ed. Washington, D.C.: National Training Laboratories, 1967.

Patterson, J. Wilbur, *Simulation Games: Media and Methods for Lay Education.* Philadelphia: Geneva Press, 1969.

Shaftel, F. R. and G. *Role-Playing for Social Values,* Englewood Cliffs, N. J.: Prentice Hall, Inc., 1967.

Simulation Games for the Social Studies Classroom. New York: The Foreign Policy Association, 1968.

Simulation Games

Blacks and Whites. Psychology Today, Educational Products Division, P.O. Box 4762, Clinton, Iowa. (Where to buy property in a city.)

The Cities Game. Psychology Today, Educational Products Division, P.O. Box 4762, Clinton, Iowa. (Four groups attempt to form coalitions to solve problems.)

Democracy. Washington, D.C.: 4-H Club Foundation.

The Decision-Making Model. Philadelphia: World Affairs Council of Philadelphia. (Game relating to international affairs.)

Dignity. New York: Friendship Press. (Game on human relations with a setting in the black ghetto.)

Games People Play. Locust Valley, New York: Adult Leisure Products Corporation. (Game based on book by Eric Berne of the same name as the game.)

Generation Gap. Baltimore, Maryland: Academic Games Project. (Game dealing with relationships between parents and adolescents.)

Ghetto. Western Publishing Company, New York. (Persons seek to improve themselves and their neighborhood.)

Life Career. Baltimore, Maryland: Academic Games Projects. (Game assisting in planning the best life possible for an eight-year span of an imaginary person.)

Napoli. La Jolla, California: Western Behavioral Sciences Institute. (Game dealing with national politics.)

Plans. La Jolla, California: Western Behavioral Sciences Institute. (Game dealing with changes in American Society.)

Sensitivity. Psychology Today, Educational Products Division, P.O. Box 4762, Clinton, Iowa. (Players role play from data in the dossiers of troubled individuals.)